LZ BINGO

Reid F. Tillery

LZ BINGO

Collingwood Publications, LLC
P.O. Box 926
Melrose, Florida 32666-0926

Published in the United States of America

Printed in the United States of America

ISBN 978-0-96342-973-5 (print)
ISBN 978-0-96342-974-2 (eBook)

Library of Congress Control Number: 2019907400

Dedicated to the men of Delta Company,
1st Battalion / 14th Infantry,
and especially to those who paid
"the last full measure of devotion."

ACKNOWLEDGMENTS

To Bill Boe who provided an in-depth, first-hand account of life in the boonies for an American infantryman during the Vietnam War.

To Sam Agius who filled me in on events at LZ Brillo Pad.

To Stephen Forgey who helped me get the facts straight about certain events described in this book

To Sue Tillery, my dear wife of 47 years, for listening countless times to my reading aloud the things written herein, and for her tireless and enthusiastic editing of my manuscript.

NOTE TO THE READER

Capturing history in words is not an easy task, but that was my intention when I wrote this book. My goal has been to describe accurately what took place. This book, therefore, expresses the hard, cold realities of a dirty, grimy, sweaty, bloody, kill-or-be-killed war.

The language used herein expresses those realities, including racial pejoratives used to describe the enemy. The astute reader will understand that extending verbal charity to those intent on killing you is not something most of us can or will do. Linguistically dehumanizing the enemy has likely been part of warfare for as long as people have fought. What people say about the enemy in times of war must not negatively reflect on them later in times of peace.

TABLE OF CONTENTS

INTRODUCTION

During the years 1967 and 1968, the Vietnam War was in full swing, with over 500,000 American troops in South Vietnam. Young William K. (Bill) Boe, age 21, was one of those half million. He served honorably in the U.S. Army infantry, was twice wounded, rose to the rank of Sergeant E-5, and experienced events that made him older than his years. In spite of his wounds, he finished his tour of duty, never losing his spirit or his sense of humor. Intending to become a journalist, he documented his memories in photographs, in letters to friends and family, and in his keen mind.

Having been Bill's friend since childhood, I used to encourage him to write his story. "Tell people what it was like to be a grunt soldier in Vietnam," I would say. "There are plenty of historical records for the academicians, tell the human interest story, as I know you can do. Give the folks the on-the-ground experience from your eyes and ears. Tell them what you saw and heard."

One day in 2017, we started talking about a particular incident that happened to him in Vietnam in 1968. The story was so compelling, I volunteered to write an article about it. Once I started writing the article, I knew I had to tell his whole story, if he so agreed. He did, and it has been an honor to capture in words what he and so many men like him went through in Vietnam. I've spent countless hours interviewing him, asking questions, listening to answers, asking and listening more. This book, which resulted largely from those interviews, and partly from my own research, strives to depict Bill's experience in the form of a novel, but this isn't fiction. What's portrayed here actually happened.

What's more, Bill's story is the story of many who served in Vietnam during that time. The places they were stationed might have been different, but their experiences likely had a lot in common.

One purpose of this book is for the reader to vicariously glimpse through Bill's story the realities of ground combat, and to understand to some extent what everyday life in the boonies was like for a ground-pounding infantryman.

The main purpose is to honor the good men who served with Bill, both those who made it home, and those who did not. They put their lives on the line because their country asked them to. There is no greater sacrifice than this. My sincere hope is that their sacrifice is never forgotten.

CHAPTER 1. ON LZ BINGO

Bill's eyes opened around dawn. He had spent the night on the orange clay ground, sheltered only by the poncho liner he managed to wrap around himself. As nights in Vietnam go, this one hadn't been too bad. There were no firefights, no incoming mortar rounds, no dinks trying to overrun the perimeter. Just quiet. It was a break from the repeated mortar fire raining down on them at LZ Brillo Pad, some five klicks to the west. Bill's entire company, Delta Company, had been mercifully removed from Brillo a week earlier to this new location, a slight hilltop along an obscure ridgeline, now known as LZ Bingo. Delta Company's presence here was supposed to be a well-deserved furlough from the intense enemy fire they had endured for nearly one month at Brillo.

So far, that was indeed the case. After deliberately avoiding the enemy by means of a slow, but stealthy creep down the jungled southwest slope of LZ Brillo pad, Delta Company was picked up in the wide open by armored personnel carriers, and transported almost all the way to Bingo. Bill figured this place must be pretty secure if the Army allowed them to ride in the open. Leaving the armored vehicles, the company humped the last 500 or 600 hundred meters to the hilltop, their current position.

On this day, Bill knew his platoon, Second Platoon, had been ordered to leave on a three-day mission to "search the area and try to snatch a prisoner." Long-range reconnaissance patrols called LRRPs, and pronounced "lurps," whose job it was to sneak around the jungle and find out what the enemy was up to, had reported light enemy use of nearby trails. Battalion Command wanted a live POW in hopes they could get more info on enemy operations in the area. Bill knew this meant they were to set up an ambush, hope the NVA would walk into it, and try to bring one back alive.

As a 21-year-old Platoon Sergeant, Bill was second in command only to First Lieutenant Jim Haas, the Platoon Leader. Bill knew he would be largely responsible for the safety and security of the 30-man platoon as they left the Company perimeter. Thoughts of the next few days weighed on Bill's mind as he ate his boonie breakfast, consisting of a canned roll from his C-rations, smeared with peanut butter and pineapple jelly, and washed down with grape Kool-Aid from his canteen.

Bingo wasn't nearly as secure as was Brillo Pad. At least on Brillo Pad there were heavily fortified bunkers--large hand-dug holes topped by strong planks of metal covered with numerous layers of sandbags. In a mortar attack, you could take refuge in those bunkers, and stand a good chance of surviving even a direct hit. But Bingo was a cherry new LZ, and there were no such places to hide. A few days ago, this nondescript hill-top had been covered with bamboo and bushes, which the Company had cleared out to set up a perimeter. Unlike other, more secure, perimeters, the outer limits of Bingo had no concertina wire. Groups of four men each, strung out about 50 feet apart to enclose a circle about 50 meters in diameter, guarded the perimeter. For added security outside and around the perimeter, the men set up Claymores each night. These were small mines weighing only three-and-a-half pounds. Designed to blow mostly in one direction, each Claymore had a 100-foot wire running from it back to a trigger detonator controlled by some grunt along the perimeter. Anytime someone got within range, all it took was one squeeze on the trigger, and boom! Hundreds of small steel balls went flying. Anybody within 50 meters of the front of an exploding Claymore was as good as dead.

For personal protection, most of the guys had dug for themselves small man-sized holes about two feet deep, just big enough to crawl into in hopes of avoiding small arms fire and flying shrapnel. Sometimes, they slept in their holes. Sometimes, they slept outside of them, under a poncho or two strung up to make a quickie shelter called a hooch. And sometimes they did what Bill had done. They curled up on the ground, under the wide tropical sky.

At one end of LZ Bingo the men had cleared a helicopter landing zone, thus the name LZ. Helicopters, or "choppers" as they were called, were the workhorses and warhorses of the military in Vietnam. They ferried men and supplies all throughout the country, and provided close fire support to help beat back the enemy. A Medevac chopper was called a "DUSTOFF," which stood for Dedicated Unhesitating Service to Our Fighting Forces. In Nam a chopper was often your ride in, and dead or alive, your ride out. There were hundreds of LZs dotting South Vietnam's countryside, nodes in a massive military network. Some LZs were permanent, others temporary. Some had artillery, and were often called firebases. Others like Bingo served only as a ground position for troops and a place for choppers to land.

In the center of Bingo's perimeter was the Command Post, or CP. The CP consisted of a hole in the ground, encircled by several layers of sandbags. The CP was usually inhabited by the Company Commander, a Radio Telephone Operator or "RTO" for short, and a medic. From this location, First Lieutenant Terry Bender, Delta Company's commander took charge of operations.

Bender was a product of the Army's Officer Candidate School, otherwise known as "OCS." While in Basic Combat Training, he had been selected to test for OCS. In spite of having no college degree and no former service, he soon found his young butt undergoing "six months of sheer terror" at Fort Benning's Infantry School. At the end of it all, he was a fresh, new 22-year-old Second Louie, all 165 pounds of him. Now, some 19 months later, as a First Lieutenant, he made life-and-death decisions for the 80 or so men under his command.

The RTO was said to be like the Commanding Officer's (CO) personal assistant. Sometimes, as RTO, you were called on to fill in for your CO if he got disabled. You had to be able to read maps, call in air strikes and medevacs, and pretty much anticipate what needed to be done.

The radio's official Army name was a PRC-25, but everybody called it a Prick 25, or just a Prick. About the size of a case of beer, and weighing close to 25 pounds, the radio was the unit's lifeline to the outside world. Under ideal circumstances, it had a maximum range of about 18 miles, but the normal range was about three to four miles. It was used to call in fire support, medevacs, or requests for supplies. The radio's heavy batteries usually lasted only a day or so. A Prick 25 was a tough piece of gear, except for its handset, which would crap out if it got wet. In the field, the RTO's antenna stuck up like a "come-and-get-me" flag. The dinks looked for it, so they could take him out. With no radio, they knew a field unit was all but screwed.

Medics were the battlefield equivalent of what we now know as 9-1-1. Injured troops would call for a medic, who'd often risk his life to get to them. Medics had been well trained at Fort Sam Houston, Texas to handle battlefield trauma in addition to numerous and diverse health factors that might affect the men—dehydration, jungle rot, immersion foot, or heat stroke. They were a walking pharmacy, dispensing malaria pills, Darvon for pain, diarrhea pills, aspirin, and a variety of other meds. Medics wielded a lot of power. If a medic determined you needed to be medevacked out, you caught the next DUSTOFF to the rear. Even a General couldn't override a medic's judgment. The troops had great respect for the medic, and often referred to him as "Doc." He was, after all, the closest thing to a doctor most of them would see in the field. A medic's main job was to keep a wounded or severely ill soldier alive until a DUSTOFF could swoop in to deliver him to more definitive medical care in the rear.

On this seventh day of June, 1968, young infantry Sergeant William K. (Bill) Boe of Pahokee, Florida, a University of Georgia temporary drop-out, found himself smack in the middle of the Vietnam War, on this hill nobody had ever heard of, called LZ Bingo. Assigned to Second Platoon of Delta Company, 1st Battalion, 14th Infantry, 3rd Brigade Task Force, 4th Infantry Division, the war for Bill was about to go from hot to a whole lot hotter.

At the Platoon CP on LZ Bingo. LT Jim Haas center. Behind him is Phillips. On the right is medic "Doc" Dennis Christensen. Shirtless soldier on the left is unidentified.

On LZ Bingo. Left to right, Stephen Forgey, Bill Boe, Arnold Lovelace, Frank Belcher.

CHAPTER 2.
THE DECISION TO ENLIST

Two years before, Bill had been a journalism student at the University of Georgia. He studied hard, and played hard. He enjoyed partying and hanging out with his friends at the Alpha Gamma Rho fraternity house at 785 South Milledge Avenue. Bill had always been a natural leader, and had tended to get involved in a lot of community activities. He was opinionated and outspoken, but his outspokenness was tempered by an endearing, off-beat sense of humor.

During his adolescent years, he excelled in the Boy Scouts, where he served as Senior Patrol Leader, and reached the rank of Eagle, with two Palms. He could back down boys twice his size just by using his personality and his words. For some reason, they listened to him.

His Scout Troop 628 often took camping trips to a place called Fisheating Creek, in the northern Everglades region. Eight miles back in the wilderness, the boys set up their tents, ate out of mess kits, fought off mosquitoes and wild hogs, and generally learned to survive in the boonies. This was men and boys only in the rugged outdoors. At night, the troop played a game called "Capture the Flag." The boys were split into two teams, scattered out across the swamp. Each team had its own flag. The object of the game was to penetrate the other team's territory, grab their flag, and make it back across the lines to your team's territory. Sometimes, the game called for stealth and wits, and at other times for brute force. Flashlights in the dark swamp were out of the question because they'd give away your position to "the enemy." Little did Bill know at the time that the skills learned in Scouting would only a few years later play a major part in his wartime survival. Now in Vietnam, Bill reflected on those years and understood how much he had learned from fun and games.

Before coming to the University of Georgia in 1966, Bill spent a year-and-a-half at the University of Florida, where he took the ROTC courses required of all male students. He learned close order drill and the manual of arms, which later helped in Army Basic Combat Training. Increasingly dissatisfied with left-wing professors and the liberal culture that permeated the UF campus, Bill transferred to Georgia. Here things were more to his liking. He found a home among his Alpha Gamma Rho buddies, and soon got a gig writing for the sports section of the campus newspaper, The Red and Black.

In February of that year, a student organization in favor of the Vietnam War, held a rally in the Atlanta Stadium. Some ten thousand people, including Bill, attended. Dignitaries in attendance included Secretary of State Dean Rusk, Governor Carl Sanders, Senator Richard B. Russell, Senator Herman Talmadge, two Georgia Congressmen, the Mayor of Atlanta, and the President of Emory University. Entertainers included singer Anita Bryant, the Emory University Glee Club, and Staff Sergeant Barry Sadler who appeared in his dress greens and his green beret. He stood erect, and began to sing his signature song "Ballad of the Green Beret." The only line Sadler got to sing by himself was the very first, "Fighting soldiers from the sky…" After that, the enthusiastic audience was on their feet, singing right along, "…fearless men who jump and die…" The moment was moving and memorable. Bill took it all to heart.

A few months later, in the fall, Bill heard that an entire rifle company was wiped out in Vietnam. He became aware of the contrast between his life and the life of those at war. While he was going to class, partying at the frat house, and hanging out with cute Georgia girls from Macon and Savannah, he knew guys his age were off fighting and dying somewhere to contain the spread of communism. He was having fun, and they were off fighting. It didn't seem fair. He felt he wasn't doing his share. Some of his high school buddies were already off fighting, and here he was enjoying the cushy college life thanks to a 2-S draft deferment that let college students slide. He thought of the honorable World War II vets he had known growing up. They did their part. It was time, he thought, for him to do his.

Upon enlisting in the Army, he specifically requested to be in the infantry. His selected military occupational specialty, or "MOS," was 11B, or Eleven Bravo, as they say. This was the one most guys wanted to avoid. It was the one often given to draftees, who had no choice as did enlistees as to MOS. An 11B MOS most likely meant he'd spend a long year humping heavy gear through South Vietnam's jungles and rice paddies. If he was lucky, he'd come home. If he was luckier still, he'd come home in one piece. Folks tried to tell him he was crazy. They didn't know what had gotten in to him. They had some idea what he was in for, but they weren't inside his mind. They didn't understand his calling.

Bill took the oath of enlistment on 13 January 1967 in Hialeah, Florida and was flown to Fort Benning, Georgia to begin what every Army enlistee must endure: Basic Combat Training, eight weeks of transitioning from civilian to soldier. As one First Sergeant explained it, "You don't belong to you anymore. Your ass belongs to the United States Army."

CHAPTER 3.
BASIC COMBAT TRAINING

Basic was a flurry of military instruction—close order drill, manual of arms, physical training, the confidence course, marksmanship and required qualification with the M-14 rifle, hand-to-hand combat, bivouac, bayonet training, throwing hand grenades, land navigation, first aid, the infiltration course, and chemical-biological-radiological warfare. Bill had no problems except for the parallel bars. The Army insisted everyone be able to go hand-over-hand down a total of about 70 bars. At first, Bill could only do 10, but he worked at it, and eventually got better.

Bill's Drill Sergeant was a Sergeant King, one huge dude who looked like an NFL star with big yellow eyes. His stare could really creep you out. He was a real bad-ass, and you didn't want to get on his wrong side.

As fate would have it, Bill's company was up for a periodic inspection by none other than the Inspector General. This was a big deal. Everything had to be perfect, or there'd be hell to pay. Sergeant King wanted to take up a one-dollar-each collection among his troops to rent a buffer to polish the floor in the barracks. Hardly anyone liked to idea of giving up a dollar, considering they only made $97 per month. Sergeant King explained in his eloquent drill-sergeant way that if they were too fucking cheap to rent a fucking buffer, they could spend all fucking night hand-rubbing the fucking floor. Down deep, though, King wanted that buffer because he wanted his barracks to look good for the inspection.

Private Boe and a few of his friends, not wanting to spend all night working on a floor, derived a scheme. That night, Boe led a raid, the mission of which was to steal a buffer from one of the barracks in the reception station, on the far side of busy, four-lane US Highway 27. Those barracks contained brand new troops, still in civilian clothes. They hadn't been in the Army more than a day, so they were a soft target. Boe's "commandos" as they became known, explained to the new recruits that the Colonel had ordered them to retrieve the buffer for polishing the floors in Headquarters. When the guys hesitated to turn over their buffer, Boe's group said something to the effect of "Look, we don't want to be doing this shit anyway. We'd rather be drinking beer at the PX. All we know is the Colonel said to come get your buffer, because he wants his damned floors polished. So, here we are. If you won't give it us, then YOU go explain to the Colonel why his floors ain't getting done." The scheme worked. Boe's group liberated the buffer, carted it across the four-lane highway, a half-a-mile or so back to the barracks, sneaking it past Sergeant King's room.

When morning came, King wanted to know where the hell that buffer came from. Bill truthfully told him they had stolen it from another building on the post. "You needed a buffer. We saw it as our job," said Private Boe "to adapt and improvise to accomplish our mission, which we did, which is why you have a buffer." King did not like the idea of having a hot buffer around. Still, he liked the fact that his barracks had the only buffer in the company. That meant he and his men could look good. The Sergeant ended up keeping the buffer, and even bragged to other NCOs about his raiders.

At the end of Basic, Bill got promoted from Private E-1 to Private E-2 because of the leadership demonstrated in the buffer episode.

CHAPTER 4. TIGER LAND

After Basic, came what's known as AIT, or Advanced Individual Training. This is where you learn the skills of your assigned MOS. There are dozens of such skills in the Army. Before leaving Basic, each man checked the posted company rosters on the outside wall of the barracks to learn of his assigned MOS, and his next duty station. Some were thrilled to get jobs as postal clerks, or a similar cushy assignment that might cause them to be sent to Germany, or other desirable post. Others moaned to discover their assigned MOS was 11B-Infantry, and their next duty station was none other than Tiger Land, at Fort Polk, Louisiana.

Known as the "BIRTHPLACE OF COMBAT INFANTRYMEN FOR VIETNAM," Fort Polk's Tiger Land was considered by many to be the toughest infantry training the Army had. The whole place was designed to mimic as much as possible the hot, wet, bug-ridden, snake-infested jungles of Vietnam. The training at Tiger Land was grueling, but it was designed to teach a man to survive and win in battle. General William Westmoreland once remarked that the best infantry troops in Vietnam came from Tiger Land. If you were sent to Tiger Land, you were all but certain your next stop was Vietnam. Since Bill had signed up for 11B, and had volunteered for Vietnam, he was headed straight to Tiger Land.

There was no break between Basic and AIT. At 0600 the following morning, about five green Army buses loaded with brand-new Basic Training graduates pulled out of Fort Benning, bound for Fort Polk's Tiger Land—a specially designated sector within the post. That evening at dusk, the buses pulled under the large, overhead Tiger-Land sign. As the troops exited the buses, training Sergeants ushered them to their barracks.

Bill's records included the fact that he'd had two-and-a-half years of Army ROTC in college, and also that he had demonstrated some sort of leadership skills in Basic Combat Training. The Army therefore offered him the opportunity to attend "The Fort Polk Academy," two weeks of specialty small-team leadership training. Although it meant spending two extra weeks in Tiger Land, Bill took it. The way he saw it, those two weeks would put him ahead of the game in AIT. He also figured, if he was going to be in a shooting war, maybe a skill or two he learned at the Academy would help him survive.

To his pleasant surprise, the Academy was run like a Junior College. There were classes, and the atmosphere was professional and academic. Trainees endured none of the usual harassment bullshit so often encountered in Basic. Instructors included veteran combat soldiers, both officer and enlisted. Some had been in the Ia Drang Valley with the First Cavalry Division. A First Cav "Black-horse" patch and a CIB on a man's uniform most likely meant he'd survived the Ia Drang. "CIB" stood for "Combat Infantryman's Badge" and signified that a soldier had been in active ground combat while in the infantry. Everyone knew that a man who'd survived the fierce battle of the Ia Drang Valley must have his shit together. So, it was a good idea to pay close attention to what he had to say.

The academy's intention was to train small-team leaders for Vietnam. Future combat Squad Leaders, fire-team leaders, and Platoon Sergeants learned essential skills such as map-and-compass work, Prick 25 radio operations, patrolling, leadership skills, and first aid. The Army recognized that Vietnam was a squad-fought war. Forget fighting in big brigades. That wasn't Vietnam. Small-team leaders were crucial to success on the battlefield. In charge of maybe ten men, the Squad Leader was considered the most important guy over there, and the academy was aimed at preparing him for the job. General Westmoreland even said Vietnam was a "Squad Leader's war."

Map-and-compass work was essential for a team leader. He had to be able to determine where his team was, and how he was going to get everyone overland to accomplish the mission, without getting his men killed or wounded in the process. Trails were often avoided because they were logical places for the enemy to set up an ambush. The team leader had to choose the best, and he hoped, the safest route, and then navigate properly.

The ability to read a map and operate a radio meant you could call for air support, medevacs, or resupply choppers when needed. Calling for air support, which usually came in the form of Huey or Cobra gunships, was precise work. The enemy—either the Viet Cong (Charlie) or the North Vietnamese Army (NVA)—could be right on your ass, maybe only 30 or 40 meters distant. You knew that a couple of Cobra gunships, which could rain down hot lead, could flat-out ruin his day while saving yours. A small screw-up in plotting map coordinates, however, could mean directing fire on your own position, killing you and your men. Nobody wanted to die from enemy fire, let alone from friendly fire. It was essential the team leader be accurate with the map.

Patrolling meant being in the field with a team. Sometimes, a patrol was defensive, as is the case when you were sent out to reconnoiter an area for some particular reason such as determining enemy presence. At other times, patrolling could be offensive, such as when you were ordered to set up an ambush, the techniques of which were covered at the Academy.

Bill learned different types of ambushes, and the most practical places to set them up. There were the so-called "L-shaped" ambushes, best carried out on some type of flat or sloping terrain. The name "L" came from the fact that two lines of men were stretched out to form an L. The idea was for the enemy to walk right into the L, into the killing zone, where he could be fired on from two sides. In sloping terrain, it was best to have the vertical leg of the L uphill to make it harder for the enemy to attack through the ambush. Sometimes, to help ensure the enemy didn't flank around the ambush, an L had a line of men extending outward from the L's horizontal leg at a 45-degree angle.

Then there were "U-shaped" ambushes. These could be carried out on a ridge. The two legs of the U would be on either side of the ridge, shooting up at the enemy. Shooting towards an upslope wasn't ideal from the ambushers' perspective, but it meant the two flanks wouldn't be shooting at each other.

Caught in the killing zone of a properly set ambush, one had a fifty-fifty chance of survival if one lived through the first seven seconds. Ambushes are designed to be deadly, and that statistic proves the point. When caught in an ambush, often your best hope for living to see another day is to charge directly into the fire. While that's not an attractive option, it's all you've got.

They say "misery loves company," and men on patrol tend to bunch up in dangerous situations. Bunching up, however, is the wrong thing to do. If one man steps on a land mine, for instance, as many as five or more may be killed if they're close together. Spread out, however, casualties are likely to be fewer. If walking into an ambush, the advantage of having men spaced some distance apart instead of crowded together is obvious. The unit leader has to know enough to keep his troops spread out.

Other patrolling skills hammered into Bill's head included how to set up a night-time defensive perimeter. When stopping for the night, security was necessary in case the unit was attacked. Ideally, the unit would be on higher ground. In war, it's almost always best to be fighting from high ground. Three men to a single fighting position, each placed in a more-or-less circular, oval, or maybe even square pattern around the rest of the unit, made up the perimeter. At each fighting position, two men slept while one remained awake. Most light-weapons infantrymen were armed with an M-16, a relatively small, lightweight rifle which could be fired on either semi-automatic or fully automatic, at the touch of a selector switch. M-16s were normally loaded with a 20-round magazine.

Each platoon had two M-60 machine guns, hand-held, belt-fed weapons that shot a powerful 7.62 mm NATO round. These two guns were placed in the perimeter fighting positions where the largest number of enemy were likely to approach. If, for example, a draw led into your position, that draw was probably a good place to position an M-60.

Besides the M-60, each platoon had two M-79 grenade launchers, also called "bloop guns," because of the peculiar sound they made when fired. An M-79 looked like a single-shot, fat-barreled, sawed-off shotgun, which fired grenades, smoke rounds, illumination rounds, buckshot, and others. Naturally, these useful weapons were placed strategically along the perimeter.

What gave the perimeter its greatest strength were Claymores and trip flares located outside the perimeter. Normally, these were placed about 100 feet in front of the fighting positions, with the Claymores placed behind the flares. Trip flares had a thin, almost invisible trip wire strung low-down, and extending out several feet from the flare. In the black night, if the enemy managed to trip a flare, it would light up the area for a few seconds, giving a Claymore man time to squeeze the trigger connected by the long wire to his mine, destroying anybody within 50 meters in front of it.

When an entire company is together, "listening posts" (LPs) might be set up. Three men would be positioned together in various places about 50 meters outside the perimeter. If they heard or saw someone, they were to go back and tell the unit. Platoon-sized perimeters, however, seldom involved listening posts.

Firing at night gave away your position, allowing your attackers to zero in on your muzzle flashes. Nighttime assaults, therefore, were often met with hand grenades instead of rifle or machine-gun fire.

Leadership skills taught at the academy included how to get people to do what they don't want to do. Take walking point, for instance. The point man is the guy walking some distance up front from the rest of the patrol. If the unit is about to walk into an ambush, the hope is the point man will spot it, and help prevent the entire patrol from walking into it. Of course, the point man stands a good chance of getting killed at this time, so it's not something everyone wants to do. How do you get a man to walk point when he doesn't want to? You tell him it's his turn, and to get up there, and do his job, just like others have done. But you use judgment in picking a point man to start with. You consider size, ability, psychological make-up and other factors such as stealth and weapons skills.

First aid was an obviously important skill for a combat infantryman. The Academy didn't train people to be medics, but a leader normally carried bandages, foot powder, and pills, and had to be able to fill in as best he could for the medic, if the medic wasn't around.

These warrior skills taught at the academy gave Bill and his 100 or so fellow cadets essential knowledge that would help them prevail in Vietnam. At the very least, the skills they learned could mean the difference between dying, and living to fight another day, eventually making it back home. The Academy gave them a sobering glimpse into warfare, and what they would be called on to endure in the upcoming months.

After graduation, buses took Academy graduates several miles to their assigned barracks to begin AIT. Greeted by the yells of training sergeants, Bill knew this was going to be worse than Basic. In fact, AIT was like Basic on steroids. Gone was the pleasant atmosphere of the Academy. Bill was once again immersed in the harsh training environment he knew at Basic.

"EVERY MAN A TIGER," read the painted sign at Tiger Land. "AGGRESSIVENESS AND FIREPOWER WILL WIN," said another. The Army's intention was not only to train the soldier in advanced infantry tactics, but to instill in him a fighting spirit. Guys at Tiger Land had been civilians just three months before. At the end of their time here, they had to be prepared for combat in Vietnam.

Bill's day started early, as did all his days in Basic and AIT. Reveille formation was at 0600, meaning you had to be up and dressed by that hour, boots on, and ready for whatever was in store for that day. Sometimes, Bill's platoon didn't get back to their old wooden World-War-II-era barracks until after midnight. On bivouacs, they remained in the field, sleeping in poncho hooches, and eating C-rations, as they'd soon be doing in Vietnam. Days were spent doing physical training, or "PT" as it was called, learning to maintain and fire light-infantry weapons, including the M-16 rifle and the M-79 grenade launcher, digging bunkers, setting up Claymores and trip flares, and using a map and compass.

Another aspect of training, Escape and Evasion, called "E&E", was designed to teach a soldier how to avoid enemy capture, and if captured, how to get away. Training NCOs called "aggressors" played the enemy. They all had done a stint in Vietnam, and many were First Cav survivors of the Ia Drang Valley. When it came to warfare, Ia Drang survivors were the best of the best because they had survived the worst of the worst. They knew what their trainees might face in Nam. To make the training as realistic as possible, the aggressors intended to strike fear into their trainees. The E&E exercise was set up like a game, if you could call it a game. The pretense was that the trainees were in an enemy-infested jungle, trying to make it back to a friendly LZ. If the aggressors managed to capture them, they took the trainees to a mock POW camp, where they were "interrogated." Aggressors were allowed to physically bruise trainees, but they weren't allowed to break bones or knock out teeth. The prospect of actually being beaten added adrenalin to the game.

One of Bill's fellow trainees was a Native American called "Chief," the nickname given to almost all American Indians. Bill knew the exercise would be over at two in the morning, when they'd blow whistles to call people in. Bill told Chief he was going to find himself a nice dark cypress swamp, and quietly hide there until the game's end. Chief joined him in his plan, and the two made themselves as comfortable as possible next to a Cypress tree in a snake-infested Louisiana swamp. Somehow, the snakes weren't as threatening as what would happen to them if they got caught. As they hid there, other guys traveled in small groups, and were captured in the process. Bill and Chief, however, remained by their cypress tree, eating candy bars and waiting for the whistles, which finally came. Bill's plan worked. He and Chief never got caught. The guys who did had it pretty rough, evidenced by their black eyes, busted lips, abrasions, and other wounds.

The days at Tiger Land were long and grueling. Up before daylight, you double-timed everywhere. "Double-time" is Army talk for "run, don't walk." Meals were normally a quick 15-minute affair in the mess hall where you wolfed down whatever they served. Guys had to growl like tigers. To Bill, it all seemed like a fraternity initiation gone bad. The whole thing might have been comical, if the end goal hadn't been to prepare for a win-or-die war. After eight hellacious weeks that seemed more like months, Bill's days at Tiger Land came to a close. He was finally going home, at least for a while. It was now mid-May. This would be his first leave since he took the oath of enlistment back in January.

Tiger Land at Fort Polk, Louisiana

Where men become infantrymen

CHAPTER 5.
SAYING GOOD-BYE TO THE WORLD

Bill flew home, landing at Palm Beach International Airport, only 40 miles from his home town of Pahokee. The Army had given him two glorious weeks of freedom. No reveille formation. No waiting in line at the mess hall. No inspection. No Army stuff at all. He planned to relax, and visit with friends.

Even though he was only 20, he was more mature than his years. While most of his friends concerned themselves with high-school affairs, college credits, new cars, and other day-to-day issues, Bill knew he had a war waiting for him. Now trained in jungle warfare, he also knew what that meant. Facing the real possibility he'd never return, he was determined to make the most of his time off.

His mother was of course happy to see him. Any mother who raises a son has to be comforted to know he is alive and well. Beulah Boe was a fourth-grade elementary school teacher, who had been widowed about five years prior. Bill spent a week-end with her before she had to go back to work on Monday.

He also spent several days with three high-school buddies, now college students, who had a duplex apartment near Palm Beach Jr. College in Lake Worth. They mostly did guy things, and reminisced about old times. Four attractive girls from Belle Glade, Florida, whom he also knew from high-school, lived next door. After five months of looking at dirty, ugly-ass guys dressed in olive green, their sweet-smelling, pleasant female company was more than welcome.

Bill spent a few evenings at the bowling in alley Belle Glade, a sister small town some 11 miles from Pahokee. Its bowling alley was the happening place. You could knock down pins, eat pizza, and meet friends. He did all that.

During his time at home, he met several times with one particular girl, a tall, cute perky blonde with whom he had been close friends for a while. They found quiet, private places to talk about things, mostly who's where, and who's doing what. After putting up with the hardships of Basic and AIT, her soft touch and sweet kiss were things to treasure.

Bill had always been a Methodist, and was a life-long member of the little Methodist Church in Pahokee, where he knew almost everyone, and almost everyone knew him. While on leave, he attended services there. He got lots of handshakes, hugs, and well-wishes from people he had always known.

When it came time to leave, his high-school buddies took him to the airport. Other friends showed up as well. He remembered everyone gathered around him to shake his hand, give him a hug, and say their good byes. One young lady who showed up, he hadn't known for long at all. She walked up to give him a hug, and then to his great surprise, planted a long, slow, passionate kiss on him that he often thought about during his time in Vietnam. It was like her enduring, sweet gift to a soldier who might never come home. He then turned and walked onto the plane, bound for Seattle.

CHAPTER 6. FORT LEWIS

Fort Lewis, Bill's next duty station, was only 40 miles from Seattle. It was a refreshing change from Fort Polk. The weather was crisp. There were mountains instead of swamps. And the intensity of the place was much less than that at Tiger Land. Some of his old Fort Polk buddies were there, but there were also a lot of new guys from places like Fort Ord and Fort Jackson. They received six weeks of additional training at Fort Lewis. A lot of it he had done before, but this time it wasn't so intimidating. They did PT, practiced patrolling, hand-to-hand combat, and land navigation. They even had an Escape and Evasion course, but it was a cake walk compared to what he and Chief had been through at Tiger Land.

All in all, he liked Fort Lewis. It was mostly an 8-to-5 life. You trained until five o'clock, then you were free. He used his time off to explore places like Chinatown in Seattle, and visit with Calvin Spooner, an old friend from home, now living in Kent, Washington.

At the Fort Lewis PX, he bought a Kodak Instamatic camera for $18. He thought it was expensive, but being a journalist at heart, he knew he had to have it. Besides, it was the camera of choice in Vietnam because it would fit perfectly into a Prick 25 battery pack. It was durable, functional. It shot prints or slides. He ended up carrying it all over Vietnam.

His other in-country treasures included a small transistor radio given to him by his Aunt Kathryn, and a Buck sheath knife Mr. Robert Simonson from back home had given him before he left. Bill's father, Hugo Boe had died in an auto accident some five years earlier. At the tender age of 16, it was a bad time in Bill's life to lose his father. Mr. Simonson gave him that knife as a sign of love, respect, and caring because he knew Bill didn't have a father to demonstrate those things to him. Simonson also gave him one other thing—a good-luck silver dollar he had personally carried in World War II. He instructed Bill to keep this dollar coin, and to bring it back to him when he came home. One other thing Bill carried was a small Confederate flag bought in Atlanta, which he tucked into his helmet liner. Of course he loved the American flag, but as a Southerner and student of history, he loved the Confederate flag as well. It showed he was not just an American. He was an American from the South. So, in his rucksack, along with water, C-rations, ammo, grenades, and Claymores, he always carried the camera, the radio, the knife, the silver dollar, and the Confederate flag.

Bill at Fort Lewis, Washington

CHAPTER 7. THE LONG VOYAGE

At the end of their stay at Fort Lewis, Bill and many others were loaded onto Army buses which took them to Tacoma, where their troop ship was docked. The USNS Upshur, would take them all the way to Vietnam. Before their arrival at port, however, they were instructed to remove the 25th Infantry patches from their uniforms. The enemy watched U.S. troop movements carefully. The Army knew there'd be spies who'd report which division was gaining additional troops, and how many. Without patches, Charlie and the NVA had no way of knowing who they were, or exactly where they were headed. Uniforms stripped clean of insignia, they were merely soldiers boarding a ship. The enemy undoubtedly knew they were headed to South Vietnam, but had no idea where in the country they'd be. The no-patches rule remained in effect almost the whole time Bill was in Vietnam. Uniforms displayed no name, no rank, and no unit insignia. The men knew who they were, but to the enemy's spying eyes, each man was a generic soldier.

Once aboard ship, Merchant Mariners assigned them to their bunks in troop bays, each housing around two hundred men. With that many people crowded together, it got pretty warm below decks. Some troops were assigned jobs aboard the ship, while others were able to relax and enjoy the ride. As luck would have it, jobs were given out in alphabetical order. Bill, whose last name starts with a "B," was near the top of the list, so he was assigned the joyous task of working eight hours each day in ship's laundry.

On the way to Vietnam, the ship stopped in Okinawa. Bill got a day pass, and went to the enlisted men's club where he drank Olympia beer, and listened to a Filipino band sing about going to San Francisco and wearing flowers in your hair. He knew he wouldn't be in San Francisco any time soon. It was all so surreal. On the way back to the ship, he walked through sugar cane fields. They reminded him of home in South Florida, where sugar cane grew in abundance. That night he sat on deck, and stared at Okinawa, so far from home. He felt as if he were on some great adventure, but he still had a long way to go.

Several days later, late in the evening, the coast of Vietnam came into view. The ship was sailing south, maybe a mile or two off shore. Bill recalled how they stood that night on the starboard side, drinking coffee and Cokes from the ship's canteen, and gazed at the mainland. There were a few lights from scattered coastal villages, but mostly the land was dark. The darkness, however, would be interrupted now and then by distant illumination flares, and the far-off thundering of artillery. They had just experienced their first sights and sounds of war. Something was going on up in those hills. Was someone battling for their lives? Would they soon join them in a similar fight? Still, the group mood wasn't exactly somber. They had trained for war for months, and were mostly confident they could do what they were trained to do.

While still aboard ship, the troops found out via an announcement, that they wouldn't be assigned to the 25th Infantry Division after all. They would be joining the 4th Infantry Division. Upon hearing this, a collective groan went up. The 4th, they knew, was taking heavy casualties in the Central Highlands. In fact, back in Fort Lewis, they had called those assigned as replacements to the 4th "the walking dead." Now, they themselves had to take on that name.

When Bill woke up the next morning, the ship was already moored in Qui Nhon's harbor. After breakfast, he grabbed his duffel, and waited on deck with the others to disembark. They watched the comings and goings of small-boat traffic. These weren't the familiar ski craft and fishing boats he'd grown up around. These boats, each long and covered with a low thatched roof, were obviously Asiatic. Seeing them all around was clear evidence he was a long way from home. The harbor was strewn with all sorts of floating debris, including even large barrels. The water was littered, but didn't seem particularly foul or polluted. There were Portuguese man-o-war everywhere, so many in fact, that the thought of falling overboard sent shivers down Bill's spine. He figured a guy falling in would be dead within a few minutes from their toxic stings.

After a two-hour wait, numerous landing craft, called LSTs, began to pull continually alongside the ship to ferry the troops which numbered in the hundreds, the half-mile or so to shore.

The troop ship USNS Upshur

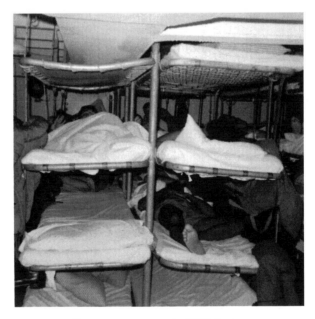

Sleeping quarters on the USNS Upshur

Soldiers begin their tour of duty on the USNS Upshur.

Soldiers preparing to disembark in Qui Nhon

CHAPTER 8. ARRIVAL IN-COUNTRY

Once ashore, they passed wounded soldiers on stretchers. One guy in particular, half-way sat up, supported by his elbow, looked at Bill and said, "My war is over. Yours is just starting. I feel sorry for you guys." He wasn't being sarcastic. There was genuine pity on his face. He was the one wounded, yet he was the one who felt sorry for them.

The large group was herded onto different buses, according to where they had been assigned. Bill's group boarded the now-familiar green Army buses, the windows of which were covered with wire grating so a hand grenade couldn't be lobbed in. The buses carried them a couple of miles or so to an open field outside of town. There, they left the buses and loaded onto two-and-a-half ton Army trucks, called "deuce-and-a-halfs."

They then traveled South Vietnam's mostly graveled Highway 1 north to Duc Pho. None of the new troops had rifles, leaving them unarmed, which made Bill feel vulnerable. One security rider rode in the back of each truck, and usually leaned alertly over the cab, where he rested his M-16 rifle. Military Police Jeeps, outfitted with M-60 machine guns, accompanied the convoy, providing at least some sense of security.

The 120-kilometer ride up to Duc Pho was mostly through flat country, with low mountains off in the distance. Bill remembered thinking how beautiful the countryside was. The terrain's lush greenery dotted with rice paddies, palm trees, and banana trees was magnificently offset against a deep, blue tropical sky. Water buffalos grazing lazily in the fields only added to what seemed to be a peaceful pastoral setting.

They went through little towns and thatched-hut dusty villages, where people were busy going about their daily lives, seemingly unconcerned they lived in a combat zone. Make-shift buildings obviously made of scrap metal and wood testified to the innovative genius of skilled Vietnamese carpenters. Such structures formed little roadside strip malls where people sold and bought items necessary for day-to-day living.

Road traffic consisted mostly of motor scooters, and small compact vehicles. Many of the scooters had a long-haired girl riding side-saddle as passenger. Bill noticed a little Catholic church with nuns, evidence of the remaining French influence in this part of the world. Somehow, a Christian church made this strange, new land seem a little less alien. He also saw little roadside pagodas used by local Buddhists. "If there weren't a war going on," Bill thought, "this would be a great place for a travel adventure."

The only evidence of war Bill saw were sandbag bunkers near bridges, staffed with guards from South Vietnam's irregulars. Different from the Army of the Republic of Vietnam, called ARVNs, these irregulars, nick-named "Powder Puffs," were more like local militia hired to guard the bridges. Armed with World War II M-1 carbines, these sentinels were tasked with keeping the bridges safe from the Viet Cong.

CHAPTER 9. DUC PHO

About five klicks from the coast, near Duc Pho was a large, dusty military encampment. Most of the structures were olive-green general purpose tents erected on wooden platforms and surrounded by low walls of sandbags. Near some of the tents, sandbag-covered bunkers promised shelter in case of mortar attacks. Jeeps, trucks, and other military vehicles rumbled by, scattering clouds of dust. The make-shift landing strip accommodated large, fixed-wing aircraft. Helicopters of all sorts—Hueys, gunships, medevacs, Chinooks—came and went.

Duc Pho was no resort by any means, but compared to the life Bill had now come to know in the field, the time spent there seemed almost cushy. For one thing, you could at least get a shower under a hanging 30-gal drum with holes punched in it, forming a slow drip. You, and perhaps several others, gathered around under the barrel, lathered up, and rinsed off. After your shower, you replaced the water you had used from the drum.

To do so, you filled a bucket from a water-bladder truck, climbed a ladder, and poured the water into the drum. The shower had a wooden-slat floor, and was screened by canvas. In the boonies, you often went weeks without bathing. When you could no longer stand your own stench, you might find time to sponge your face and creases using water poured into your steel-pot helmet.

Besides the welcomed showers, Duc Pho also had a mess hall which served hot meals, a pharmacy, a medical center, the battalion hospital, and even an enlisted men's club where a soldier could have a Ballantine or a Black Label beer. The club was a little wooden hooch that held 30 or 40 people. Outside, draped parachutes provided additional sheltered space.

For other entertainment at Duc Pho, old movies and TV shows, mostly from the 50s, maybe early 60s, were shown on the sides of buildings using a flickering projector. Bill especially enjoyed watching episodes of Bonanza and Gunsmoke.

Another of Duc Pho's relative luxuries were wooden latrines. In the boonies, an infantryman's toilet was often a cardboard box in his bunker, or behind any bush he could find where he hoped he wouldn't get shot. The convenience of the latrines came at a price, however. Somebody had to do "shit detail." Human waste from the wooden latrines went into 30-gallon drums split in half. Those on shit detail were assigned the task of pulling the drums, adding diesel to the contents, lighting it, then stirring the whole nasty mess with a long stick, as it burned. At day's end, you smelled like a combination of shit and diesel until you could shower under the drum.

Bill's assigned company, Delta Company, was born at Duc Pho, when the Army pulled men from Alpha, Bravo, and Charlie Companies to make a four-company battalion. About 100 of them had trained together at Fort Lewis, and were part of a "replacement packet" sent over on the USNS Upshur. Rather than sending individuals to filter as strangers into units here and there, the Army in this case had reverted to an old World-War-II strategy, that of training men back home as a group, and then sending them off together to fight. The idea was they'd already know one another, and for that reason could better function as a team. An additional 40 or so combat-seasoned veterans were added to the 100 cherry new guys to form Delta Company, which along with Alpha, Bravo, and Charlie, now made up the 1st Battalion of the 14th Infantry, 3rd Brigade Task Force, 4th Infantry Division. The "Task Force" designation meant Bill's group, rather than being assigned to a specific section of Vietnam, could be sent any-where the Army needed them. And the Army always needed them where the war was the hottest.

Army organizational structure is flexible in terms of numbers, but ordinarily a company might average around 130 men. Each company normally has three to five platoons, with 25 to 40 men per platoon. Each platoon is divided into squads of 6 to 10 men. Bill was assigned to Second Platoon, Delta Company. Promoted to Private First Class the moment he stepped onto Vietnamese soil, he was now an ammo bearer for an M-60 machine gunner. This meant he carried his own M-16 and ammo, all his personal gear, and the heavy, belt-fed ammo for the M-60. At only 160 pounds, he was loaded down with about 55 pounds. He remembered wondering how he'd be able to run and fight in the jungle with all this gear. A weighted-down, slow-moving GI would be an easy target for Charlie to pick off.

The two weeks at Duc Pho were dedicated mostly to in-country training. They zeroed in their newly issued M-16s, and carried them for the first time on platoon-sized patrols around the base. Although the area was fairly secure, this was technically their first patrol into enemy territory. The Viet Cong were active around Duc Pho, and although not expected where they were, they could have run into VC at any time. Although not usually active during the day here, Charlie was out at night. With the men properly spread out, the point man led the way, and flank security covered the platoon's two sides. Combat veterans supervised operations, providing tips that might help the new arrivals survive their tour of duty. They learned, for example, never to walk through a hedgerow using a trail because that's a likely spot for Charlie to plant a booby trap. Instead, they learned to find another, less likely spot, like maybe an obscure thinning in the hedge. They learned that walking the dikes through a rice paddy made them an easy target. Better to get wet walking along the side of the dike. If fired on, you may at least be able to use the dike for cover if the bullets are coming from its other side. Besides the paddies, they also patrolled the one big hill close to the base. It was wooded, and not open, giving them experience in heavy brush. Two patrols a day, most days, helped them acclimate to what awaited them in the coming months.

One glance around Duc Pho would tell you that sandbag architecture was in style here. Multiple rows of sandbags surrounded tents, other structures, and bunkers. Sandbag walls stood in front of doorways in such a way that you would have to walk around them to enter. Sandbags provided protection from mortars, bullets, and flying shrapnel. In case of an attack, layers of sandbags between you and what was going on raised your chances of survival a few notches.

Sandbag duty involved filling sandbags with dirt. Spending half a day filling sandbags was a relatively pleasant task. A refreshing cooler of Kool-Aid was usually on hand, and Vietnamese kids would sometimes come help, in exchange for candy and treats. This was Bill's first opportunity to socialize with the Vietnamese people. He especially remembered one cute, little 15-year-old beauty named Frenchy, with long, dark hair. She wanted desperately to go to America. She'd say in broken English, "I fill sandbags. You take me to United States." Of course, Bill and the guys with him wanted to go to the United States, too, but they weren't going any time soon, and they certainly couldn't take Frenchy with them.

At Duc Pho, a drunk soldier taught Bill his most important in-country lesson. Bill and perhaps thirty other men were sleeping under a large, sandbag-encircled tent with a wooden floor. They were in their mosquito-bar-covered cots, dressed only in their underwear, some tucked under a poncho liner. The tent had no lights. At about 2200 hours, the drunk walked in, and in the darkness he announced he had a few things to say, a few words of wisdom from a combat veteran, to leave behind. He said, "You're all layin' here like Victor Charlie's bait. You're in your little skivvies, and as soon as Charlie starts mortaring this place, you won't be able to find anything. You'd better keep your boots and fatigues on. This ain't no game. It ain't no Boy Scout camp. I'm going home. Some of you ain't. When the rounds start comin' in, you'll get killed looking for your pants and boots." The soldier then turned and walked out, presumably to deliver that lecture to the next tent. One guy who'd had one too many was doing his part to keep them alive.

Lying in his cot, in his underwear, Bill didn't know where his helmet was. Remembering his old Boy Scout motto, "Be prepared," he took the drunk's lesson to heart, got up, found his helmet, and put on his pants and boots. Never again in Vietnam did he remove them, except for medical care, or to change or to bathe.

General Purpose Tents at Duc Pho

Bill reads a letter from home at Duc Pho

Patrolling at Duc Pho

CHAPTER 10. CHU LAI

About 80 klicks north of Duc Pho lies the coastal city of Chu Lai, the site of a United States military base, and the home of the 196th Light Infantry brigade, who hosted Delta Company for a week of continued in-country training. The 196th had an honorable history in Vietnam, and good morale. Bill's 4th Division, on the other hand, had mixed morale. For one thing, they had a horrible Area of Operations, referred to as an "AO," in the Central Highlands. If their butts got in a battlefield bind, there were no neighboring troops to come to their rescue. Also, the 4th Infantry Division in 1967 took more casualties, and killed more enemy soldiers than any other Division.

Bill remembered the scenic hilltop classroom overlooking the South China Sea, where Delta Company learned from combat-seasoned veterans of the 196th how a platoon operated in the field, and how Squad Leaders and fire team leaders worked together. They learned additional mapping skills, and how to call in air and artillery strikes. One demonstration brought in a couple of helicopter gunships in an impressive display of how the system worked. Other classroom topics included how to distinguish the Viet Cong from regular villagers. Since the VC could blend into the general population, it was hard to tell the enemy from innocent civilians. Perhaps hiding ammo, weapons, rice, and other provisions for the NVA, some of the folks you'd see would smile at you during the day, and given half a chance, would kill you that night. You had to assume that almost everyone you met wanted to put maximum pain and suffering on you.

There were also lessons on how scout dogs work, and how to avoid trip wires by looking for clues such as footprints or snapped twigs, evidence someone had been in the area. Classes on patrolling emphasized that the group should spread out, not bunch up, and that the point man shouldn't get too far out ahead. They learned that when searching a village, one fire team provides security while the other does the probing. The 196th did their best to clue in the new guys to tricks they'd need to know to dominate on the battlefield, and survive to go home.

When not in classes, Delta enjoyed a relatively comfortable stay at Chu Lai, where they slept in clean, screened barracks, ate in a proper mess hall, bought goodies at the canteen, watched movies at night, and could visit the PX where Bill bought film for his Instamatic. The post even had its own swimming area. At week's end, Delta Company convoyed back to Duc Pho. Riding in the truck on the way back, Bill thought his time at Chu Lai was well spent.

CHAPTER 11. OPERATION BENTON II

Benton II was a search-and-destroy mission carried out west of Chu Lai. The entire battalion took part. Its purpose was simple—find the enemy, and kill him. VC would come into the area, and terrorize the villagers, making them pay portions of their rice harvest as tribute, and forcing their young men into VC service. The Viet Cong brutally and publicly murdered villagers who refused to cooperate. The South Vietnamese Army wanted the villagers removed to locations where they'd be given housing, and could be protected. Leaflets had been dropped explaining the situation. To prevent the Viet Cong from using the villages, they were to be burned. The idea was, after the war, villagers could be returned, and homes could be rebuilt.

Having been assigned to the mission, Delta Company loaded eight men each onto choppers, and headed for the field, expecting a cold assault, meaning they didn't anticipate taking fire upon landing. Once in the field, Delta Company broke into separate platoons, each platoon having been assigned its AO. Although the separate platoons were operating about a couple of kilometers apart, they never saw one another except about once every three days for half-an-hour or so, when they'd meet the resupply choppers. At those times, the company would form a defensive perimeter around the LZ, and the choppers would deliver food, water, fatigues, or whatever else might be needed. Sometimes, there'd be a big red mail bag on the chopper, which meant letters from home. That big red bag was always a welcomed sight because it might mean a letter from your family or girl-friend. They'd divide the delivered provisions, then separate into platoons to hump the boonies once again.

For a unit in the field, every two weeks choppers would bring in clean clothes--fatigue shirt and pants, undershorts, tee shirts, and socks. These were piled separately on tarps spread on the ground. Then, everyone would strip butt naked one squad at a time, pile their dirty clothes on tarps, and pick up clean ones. This had to be a quick and efficient operation. You didn't have time to check for sizes. You grabbed something and put it on quickly, because when shooting might start at any moment, you didn't want to be long without clothes on. Wearing the same clothes for two weeks meant they became wet with salty sweat, and ultimately stiff as cardboard. You had to wonder if your stench was enough to give away your position to any VC within several hundred meters.

Bill's Platoon Leader was a good guy, a Second Lieutenant about 25 years old. This was a young man's war, and young men did extraordinary things. The Lieutenant was great at reading maps, and commanding his 30 or so men. He led them on their search of their own AO, first along hedgerows, and among small huts, which by now were empty because of the mandated evacuation. In two of the structures, they found several tons of rice, obviously a food cache for NVA troops. To render the rice unusable, they spread it on the ground where the rain would soon ruin it. Using Zippo lighters, so common among the troops, they then set light to the empty dwellings, burning them to the ground, as ordered.

They went from village to village, walking trails and roads, passing civilians, some on bicycles, some leading water buffaloes. They came to one small settlement, still occupied. The people there were supposed to have left, according to the evacuation order. But this was their home, as it likely had been for generations. These were poor subsistence farmers, with no interest at all in international politics, communism, or the war. Yet, they were ripe targets for Viet Cong terrorists, which is why they had been ordered to leave. Still, they wanted to be left alone to live their lives, and were obviously intimidated by the sight of helmeted, armed-to-the-teeth soldiers around their homes. Nevertheless, the platoon had orders to burn structures, so the two small huts there were torched, while the villagers watched. Nobody felt the least bit good about what they had done.

A half mile or so down the way, they came to another small, occupied settlement. The Lieutenant said, "I need a Zippo." Nobody answered. He looked straight at one of the guys. "You gotta Zippo?"

"Sir, mine's out of fluid," was the reply.

"Who's got matches?" asked the Lieutenant.

"I don't smoke, sir," answered one.

"Okay, anybody else got matches?" asked the Lieutenant.

All he got back from his men were silent, scornful stares.

Looking at his soldiers and the villagers, he then replied "We're not burning any more villages." And they didn't.

The first war casualty Bill saw was a pregnant woman, lying dead in a rice paddy, her baby bump plainly visible. He asked his buddy Ronnie Williams what had happened to her. Ronnie didn't know for sure, but told Bill there was some crazy asshole in one of the other platoons. "He likes to shoot people. He probably shot her for target practice," said Ronnie. Bill was shocked. He didn't come here to shoot civilians. He came to fight communists trying to take over South Vietnam.

About an hour and a half later, after walking through more rice paddies, and along more hedgerows, the platoon stopped for a break. They normally liked to stop where there was cover, in case of an attack. Bill sat in a small depression in the ground. Then, all of a sudden--Zing! Zing! Zing! Bullets whizzed by to the left and to the right of his head, sounding like supersonic wasps as they tore through the air. Almost at that same instant, two or three bullet holes popped open in the thick trunk of a banana tree just to his left. A few inches were all that had separated Bill from a certain and sudden death. The shots came from thick brush perhaps 50 feet away. The shooter was no doubt VC. Judging from the semi-automatic nature of the rifle fire, the shots came from an old Soviet SKS rifle instead of the newer, fully automatic AK-47. Fortunately for Bill, Viet Cong sometimes carried older weapons and were often poor marksmen.

"Let's get the little bastard!" yelled one guy. In an impressive display of gung-ho bravery, two or three of the others in Bill's platoon took out through the bush like hounds after a rabbit. A few minutes later, several shots rang out. Shortly afterwards, the guys came back saying "The little dink bastard got away."

At that point, Don Hollenbach, one of the platoon's M-79 grenadiers, from Levittown, New York looked at Bill and said, "Congratulations, Boe." Bill thought he meant congratulations for being alive. Then Hollenbach said, "You just earned your CIB."

This was the first time Bill was shot at. Those rounds weren't fired indiscriminately at the platoon. The shooter had obviously selected Bill as the target. Having been in the field only a short time, Bill had already come close to death. He now knew the sensation of bullets ripping past his head, another step he reckoned in this whole Vietnam experience.

The platoon at this point was in VC country. The enemy in Vietnam included both the VC and the North Vietnamese Army. The VC were South Vietnamese communists organized into a clandestine force of irregular combatants who blended into the general population. Their ranks included not only military-aged men, but also old men, women, and sometimes even children. The vicious VC organization was part of life in both the cities and the villages. Anybody could be VC. Charlie might be a banker, a farmer, a teacher, a pregnant woman, anyone. You might see someone peacefully herding ducks along, or working in a rice paddy, and an hour or two later, they'd be hiding in the bushes taking shots at you. A VC might be a civilian all month, only picking up a rifle once or twice when the opportunity to shoot Americans presented itself. Non-VC who knew who the VC were, dared not give them up, for fear they themselves would be killed. After all, neither the American or ARVN soldiers were around all the time, but the VC were. The VC had the guns. The civilians didn't. Once the soldiers were gone, the VC would ruthlessly murder anyone they thought had crossed them. Ending the VC's reign of terror was one big reason Delta Company, and indeed the entire U.S. military, was in Vietnam.

The platoon spent nights in the field in any convenient clearing they could find where the terrain might offer some advantage in an attack. Always before nightfall, they set up a secure perimeter by posting gun positions around the clearing, usually with three men per position. In front of the gun positions, they readied their Claymores, and in front of the Claymores, they set out their trip flares. In the middle of the small perimeter was the CP. Here, you'd usually find the Platoon Leader, the Platoon Sergeant, the RTO, and the medic. After dark, each man in the gun positions took one-hour turns on watch, while his two buddies slept as best they could curled up on the ground with a poncho between them and any rain, and a poncho liner for warmth. They did all this for days and weeks on end, patrolling during the day, and getting any rest they could within the confines of what they hoped was their relatively secure perimeter during the long, dark, and dangerous nights.

A few days after Bill was shot at, the platoon was patrolling an area of rice paddies. The Vietnamese often terraced hillsides in such a way that the flat terraces on which the rice grew, resembled the distinct, stair-step contours of a topographic map. The patrol was spread out near and along a hedgerow at the level of the third or fourth terrace, which was elevated about 50 feet from the flat ground at the hill's base. Suddenly, they started taking rifle fire from across the paddy on the flat ground. They dove into the thin hedgerow seeking cover. To their great surprise, on the other side of the hedgerow, like a magnificent gift from God, was a proper trench! Taking cover in the relative safety of the trench, they returned fire, and in a few minutes the hostile firing ceased. For safety's sake, they remained in the trench about half an hour, using the opportunity to have a C-ration snack. While eating, they noticed graffiti on tree trunks, written in French! Apparently, they had dived into a trench that at one time had been occupied by French soldiers or Legionnaires. In 1954, after the Battle of Dien Bien Phu, the French said to hell with Vietnam, and left. Now, here in September of 1967, the men of Second Platoon, Delta Company, found themselves in the very same trench fighting more or less the same tenacious little bastards the French fought.

Second Platoon continued their daily patrolling, searching the area looking for VC, or evidence of VC, such as rice caches or weapons. They rarely saw the VC, who fought on their own terms, and were hard to identify, unless they happened to be armed and traveling in a group. While searching for the enemy, platoon members were literal walking targets for any VC who wanted to sneak around and take shots at them.

Finally, came a report over the Prick 25 from Delta 6, the radio name for the Company Commander, that there was a confirmed kill of a VC armed with an SKS rifle. The report heightened excitement among the troops for a time, because they now knew they could bring the war to the enemy. That excitement, however, was short lived. A day or two later, on 17 September, Second Platoon got word that one of Delta Company's men from Third Platoon had been shot and killed while crossing a small stream or ditch. Twenty-year-old Guadalupe Perez from San Joaquin, California, was Delta Company's first fatality.

Two days later, on 19 September, tragedy again struck Delta Company. It was early morning, and they were leaving their nighttime hilltop perimeter. VC treasure hunters would often come in behind an overnight position to police up any C-rations, hand grenades, smoke grenades, or other gear left behind. Second Platoon stayed behind to ambush any VC entering the area. When none came, orders came for them to leave the hilltop, so they left walking single file down the trail away from the area. Bill was ammo bearer for Cheek Crosslin, the machine gunner. Cheek was right behind Bill, and Ronnie Williams, assistant machine gunner, was right behind Cheek. About 50 feet down the trail and away from the hilltop, exploding mortar rounds could be heard. Sergeant Howard yelled, "Incoming! Get down!" There was a little gulley to their right. Bill dived in the gulley, and could feel Cheek just behind him. Five mortar rounds hit down the trail beside them. Then the firing stopped. Cheek was lying across Bill's legs. Bill turned his head, and said, "Cheek. You okay?" Cheek said nothing. His eyes had a blank look.

"Ronnie. I think Cheek's hit," said Bill. Bill pulled his feet out from under Cheek, and at that moment knew he was dead.

Sergeant Howard yelled from down the trail "G--dammit. That was friendly fire! We just got hit by our own mortars!"

Many times after leaving a nighttime perimeter, the area would be mortared to destroy anything left behind, so Charlie's treasure hunters couldn't have the use of it. On this day, Second Platoon was not quite out of the area when the mortar fire began.

Knowing Cheek had been killed by friendly fire, Ronnie said, "I can't take this. I've been with him the whole war. I can't believe this is how it's going to end for him."

Cheek, was Gailen Cheek Crosslin, of Midwest City, Oklahoma. He was a 20-year-old short-timer who had only two months to go in Vietnam. He counted the days by drawing little calendars on his helmet, meticulously marking off each day. He didn't care much for being in the war, and was looking forward getting back to his hills of Oklahoma. Cheek was a good Squad Leader, a good machine gunner, and a good soldier. He was a great guy to have watching your back. His bride back in Oklahoma was Patty, whom he affectionately called "Patticake." When Bill first arrived in-country, Cheek had been a mentor to him, teaching him things that might ensure survival and make in-country life easier.

There was another casualty that morning. Ammo bearer Rodney Piampiano from California received shrapnel wounds to his arm.

The call went out over the radio that Delta Company had "one Kool-Aid and one peanut," meaning one killed and one wounded. These terms were common radio code in Vietnam. They were used so Charlie, who might be monitoring the channel, wouldn't know how many casualties were suffered. Still, with code that simple, Charlie had probably figured out its meaning. They went through Cheek's ruck taking out anything that could be used in the field, such as C-rations and grenades. Cheek's personal effects stayed with him.

Within ten minutes a Huey landed. Holding one corner of the poncho used as a litter to carry the lifeless body, Bill trembled all over as they took Cheek to the chopper. It was all Bill could do to fight back tears of shock and grief. After they loaded Cheek aboard, Piampiano climbed on. The chopper then revved its engines, lifted off in a cloud of dust and debris, pulled away, and soon disappeared from sight.

A few minutes later, the platoon was again humping the boonies, as they had been doing thirty minutes earlier. Only now, Cheek was dead and gone, and Piampiano had left, never to return to Delta Company. As he walked along, Bill thought about how fragile life is. Cheek was here one minute, and gone the next. Each day, Bill thought, had to count for something. You couldn't see your days as markers to be crossed off because you never know how many you have left. Tomorrow, he had come to realize, is only a shadow, a dream, a hope. Today is what counts. No matter how bad things are, you have to make the most of today.

The platoon spent the next two days humping heavy gear through the hot and humid countryside in search of the elusive enemy. Then, on the morning of 22 September, about an hour or so after they had left the security of their nighttime perimeter, they were walking single file down a wet and slippery hillside trail. Bill was about the tenth man in line. Ronnie Williams, the new machine gunner now that Cheek was gone, walked in front of Bill, who was now assistant machine gunner. Don Hollenbach was right behind, humping the ammo, and Ota Wallace from Hawaii nicknamed "Pineapple," the generic nickname for almost any Hawaiian, was somewhere behind Hollenbach. With in-country fatigues stripped of names, ranks, and other insignia, guys were sometimes known mainly by their nicknames, as was the case with Wallace.

Bill momentarily stepped a few inches to the side of the trail in hopes of using the low trailside vegetation for better footing to keep from slipping on the wet clay. Suddenly, a great explosion enveloped Bill's whole world. He felt his body being hurled into the air off to his left. Landing about ten feet from where he had been, he lay motionless among some bushes, trying to process what had happened. He couldn't feel his right leg below the knee at all. Realizing he had stepped on a land mine, he looked at his right leg, partially hidden by brush, and couldn't see his foot.

Ronnie Williams was the first at Bill's side.

"You okay?" asked Williams.

"Where's my foot?" asked Bill.

"Well, it's right there," said Williams.

"Yeah, but is it on my leg?" asked Bill.

"Yeah it is," said Williams, who then pulled Bill's foot out of the brush. "There's blood coming out of your boot. I'm gonna take your boot off," said Williams.

Williams removed Bill's boot, and saw his foot covered with blood. He wrapped it in one of the prepackaged medical bandages each man carries.

"We gotta get you up side the hill because a chopper's gonna come get you," said Williams.

While this was going on, several guys, using machetes, cut the tall grass nearby to make a clearing for the chopper to land.

With Bill's right arm draped over Williams's shoulder, Williams helped Bill limp to the clearing. At the same time, Hollenbach carried Bill's pack.

At the clearing, Bill saw that Pineapple had also been wounded, having received severe shrapnel wounds to both thighs.

The day's third casualty was the platoon's medic whose face had been peppered with shrapnel. With blood on his face, the medic was tending to Pineapple, who was lying in the grass with his upper legs bandaged, and groaning in pain. By now, Pineapple had likely received a shot of morphine.

As the medevac chopper was coming in at a distance, they popped purple smoke to let the pilot know where to land. The routine was to tell the pilot they had popped smoke, but not to reveal its color. The pilot had to describe the smoke's color. If he picked the correct color, it was confirmed he could land. Charlie might be listening to radio transmissions, and could pop smoke to attract an unwary chopper. If Charlie didn't know what color smoke to pop, he couldn't screw with the chopper.

The noisy green medevac chopper with its distinctive white squares, each containing a prominent red cross, approached the clearing and landed. They immediately loaded Pineapple on the floor of the chopper, then Bill and the medic climbed aboard. The whole procedure took less than two or three minutes. Choppers, huge targets that they were, didn't stick around long. They were in and out quickly.

As was standard operating procedure, each man's pack, canteens, and weapons stayed behind in the field, and only his personal effects went with him on a medevac. On board the chopper, Bill had his helmet, one boot, and his ammo can containing all his personal effects.

With Pineapple on the floor being worked on by two chopper medics, Bill and the wounded platoon medic nearby, the chopper's blades began to whir faster, and it lifted off. As they gained altitude, Bill got a bird's eye view of the platoon in the field below. The chopper then began forward motion, and that spot on the earth which had held so much drama, became just a memory.

Pineapple never returned to the field. The word was he was sent to Japan, then back home. If they kept you in-country, you were likely going to stay to finish your tour. If you went to Japan, you were probably going home. The injured medic was a short-timer, so he never came back. The war for both of them was over.

Patrolling a village

Ronnie Williams

Cheek Crosslin

Cheek Crosslin, left, and Ronnie Williams take a break

Rodney Pimpiano

CHAPTER 12.
REST AND RECUPERATION

During the fifteen-minute DUSTOFF ride to Chu Lai, Bill studied the beautiful countryside below, snapping photos with his Instamatic camera. Soon, the big red crosses of the landing zone at Chu Lai came into view, and the chopper settled in for a soft landing. They took Pineapple away, and Bill never saw him after that. Bill, considered walking wounded, was loaded into a Jeep and taken to the Second Surgical Hospital, where a female Army doctor did the best she could to remove shrapnel from his ankle. They bandaged him, put a drain in his foot, shot him full of antibiotics, and sent him to a hospital bunk to heal. A medic would come in every day to check his wounds. Bill settled in to enjoy the rest from the field, reading books and enjoying the "sham" time, as the guys called it—easy duty while your days in-country ticked away.

A day or two later, he was ordered to be at his bunk at 1400 hours for a Purple Heart Ceremony, where he received the honor that recognized him for being wounded in action.

A few days later, he was discharged from the hospital, and ordered to catch a flight to Duc Pho. The airfield was about three klicks from the hospital. With no way to get there but walk, Bill hobbled on his crutches down the long dusty road to catch his plane. Here he was, still only 20 years old, half a world away from family and friends, in a war many couldn't understand, determinedly making his way painfully to his next duty station. In these situations, young men grow up fast, and Bill was already older than his years.

At the airfield, Bill boarded a C-123 Caribou for the 20-minute hop to Duc Pho, where he checked in for duty. A short time later, he was taken by Jeep to his assigned tent. Still wounded, he was to pull light duty at Duc Pho until such time as his wounds healed enough to allow him to re-join his platoon.

During the day, Bill cleaned rifles for the armorer. These were all weapons of guys who'd been wounded or killed. With all the rifles to be cleaned, it didn't take a genius to figure out how many folks were getting hurt, or worse. General Sherman said, "War is hell." These dirty rifles were a silent testimony to that fact.

During the evenings, Bill was assigned to Battalion bunker guard. Permanent bunkers surrounded the base, and four to six men were assigned to each bunker. There were cots inside, and ready-made fighting positions.

Mostly, the bunkers were staffed by "Remington Raiders," or "REMs," company-clerk types whose main job was pounding on Remington type-writers, preparing morning reports, and such. Compared to infantrymen in the field, they had it dicked. Hot chow, cold beer, movies every night. Their cushy lifestyle earned them the title among infantrymen of "Rear Echelon Mother Fuckers," or simply "REMFs."

Bill, a competent machine gunner, already experienced in combat was a welcomed addition to the bunker full of REMs. The joke among the rear-echelon boys was if their bunker was attacked, they could haul ass while Bill covered their retreat with the machine gun, since he was lame, and couldn't run anyway.

While serving as the available rear guard one night on bunker duty, Bill realized it was 2 October, his birthday. He had just turned 21.

CHAPTER 13. BRIDGE GUARD

After ten days at Duc Pho, Bill was fit enough to return to his platoon. His foot now healed, he was issued new boots, another M-16, and taken by deuce-and-a-half to rejoin Second Platoon about 30 minutes away, now assigned to guarding bridges along Vietnam's Highway 1, the main road from Saigon to Hanoi. Charlie would have loved to have blown those bridges apart, so each bridge had a bunker with a squad of eight or so men guarding it.

Compared to most infantry assignments in Vietnam, bridge guard was considered good duty. Each squad had its own residence, their bunker at the end of the bridge. In this case, it was a sandbag structure about four feet wide by twelve feet long, with a dirt floor. Not quite tall enough to stand up in, it was designed to be a protected place to sleep. There were no tables or chairs of any kind. The only items remotely qualifying as furniture were air mattresses to sleep on. Usually, a grunt soldier didn't carry an air mattress because they were too heavy and bulky. But here, air mattresses came with the bunker. With an air mattress underneath, a poncho liner on top, and a ruck for a pillow, a soldier enjoyed relative comfort at night.

About a quarter-to-a-half mile east of Highway 1, and parallel to it, ran an inactive rail bed, separated from the highway by rice paddies. Sometimes at night, Charlie would position himself on that rail bed, and take pot shots at the bridge guards. Nobody in Bill's squad got hit, but it was always unnerving to know that somebody over there might have you in his sights. Charlie's muzzle flashes were generally answered with return rifle fire, so he wouldn't get too brave in this deadly cat-and-mouse game.

After several nights of incoming sniper fire, the squad got fed up, and brought in a specialist from the company's weapons platoon, who arrived one morning with a 90-millimeter recoilless rifle. This shoulder-fired, tube-like weapon shot either canister or high-explosive rounds, sometimes called "H-E" rounds. A canister round contained hundreds of mini-darts called flechettes, and was designed primarily to stop a human-wave attack. A high-explosive round was essentially a little artillery round, which is why they sometimes called the weapon "the 90-millimeter cannon."

The specialist arrived one morning, taking care to conceal his cargo inside the bunker so traffic crossing the bridge, which surely included Viet Cong, wouldn't see what they had.

That night, the evening ritual of sniper fire commenced as usual, about an hour after dark. The specialist leveled his big gun loaded with an H-E round at the muzzle flashes, warning others to stay of out the ferocious back blast. Upon firing, flames shot out the back of the tube. A red streak of fire trailed the round across the rice paddy, making it look like a souped-up Roman candle.

The round hit the distant railroad bed with a huge explosion. The specialist turned and said, "You won't get any more shit from them tonight." After that, they never got any more sniper fire while on bridge guard.

Besides guarding their assigned bridge, Bill's squad also patrolled an area around it about one square mile. They were to look for enemy activity such as groups of men of military age, any suspicious behavior, or people in the "ville," as they called the village, storing undue amounts of food or ammo.

This type of patrolling was much easier than what they had been doing. With a bunker for a nearby home, they didn't hump the heavy loads they normally carried. They mostly took with them weapons, ammo, and water. Finally, they were traveling light, just like Charlie, who usually had an advantage when it came to items carried. U.S. troops were most often weighted down with frag grenades, smoke grenades, Claymore mines, a steel helmet, heavy boots, a poncho and liner, empty sandbags, insect repellent, C-rations, maybe a machete, and a heavy ammo can containing personal effects. Besides all these items, they toted their rifle or other weapon, ammo, and several canteens filled with water. Charlie mainly carried only a weapon, ammo, water, and rice. In lieu of heavy boots, Charlie wore light sandals. He could run like the wind through the boonies, while U.S. troops plodded along like weighted-down pack mules. Bill always wondered why the Army couldn't devise a way for them to go light, so they could fight without the burden of all the weight on their backs.

Upon rejoining his platoon at the bridges, Bill had gone back to his old job of assistant machine gunner to Ronnie Williams. Ronnie was a likeable guy with a roundish face and short, brown-to-blonde hair. At 5 feet 10, he was of average build, not skinny, not stocky. Around 21 years old, he had grown up in the piney woods around Farmerville, Louisiana, not far from the Arkansas line. Before being drafted, he had been a competent heavy-equipment operator. At home, his young wife Betty now waited anxiously for his return. He had arrived in Vietnam in March of this year, and had spent every single day in the field. Most guys were out of action for a while here and there, either by being wounded, or with some illness, jungle rot, or other weird condition picked up in-country. But not Ronnie. He was always there. In fact, he was a model soldier. He could handle a machine gun, set out Claymores and trip flares, and pretty much do anything an infantryman was called on to do. Temperate in his behavior, he was no druggie or big boozer. Bill thought if every soldier in Vietnam were like Ronnie, the war effort would go a lot better.

Ronnie's rural upbringing gave him a love for the soil and growing things. He'd often look at the Vietnamese soil and announce, "If we had dirt like this back in Louisiana, we could all get rich." Ronnie had an agrarian connection with the rural South Vietnamese people. He admired their farming skills, and took notice of how hard-working they were. As far as Ronnie was concerned, he was truly there to serve and protect them. Besides fighting off those who would terrorize them, he wanted to help them directly. He wanted to show them how they farmed in Louisiana. So, he sent home for okra and corn seeds. One day, while on patrol with the squad, Ronnie gathered three or four of the villagers together, showed them the seed packets, and began planting. The villagers understood immediately, and they helped cover the seeds. After that, when out on patrol, the squad would sometimes check with the villagers to see how the plants were growing. The villagers seemed to love Ronnie because they knew he cared about them. Both the young man from Louisiana, and the Vietnamese villagers had at least one thing in common—the love of growing things in the soil.

If the idea of the war was to win the hearts and minds of the people, Ronnie helped do just that. Not everyone in the Army was the ambassador Ronnie was. A few seemed to delight in "fucking with the folks," as the soldiers called it. In fact "Don't fuck the folks" was something troops were often reminded of. Most didn't, but there was always a real asshole here and there. One day, for example, one guy threw a Vietnamese kid off a bridge. The poor child nearly drowned before other soldiers could fish him out. Actions like that only served to create more Viet Cong out of ordinary Vietnamese.

Besides the seeds, Ronnie got a bunch of powdered milk from home to give to the Vietnamese kids. Don Hollenbach became the chief milk mixer, and every weekday morning, he would organize the milk station at the bridge, handing out canteen cups of milk to Vietnamese kids on their way to school.

Hollenbach was like that. He wanted to help wherever he could. In fact, Hollenbach often volunteered to walk point, a dangerous job most people would have gladly avoided. On patrol, the point man walked ahead of the group with the aim of spotting enemy activity before the rest of the group walked into it. Sometimes, though, Charlie was known to let the point man through before ambushing the whole bunch. In any case, the job was more than hazardous, but you could count on Hollenbach to do it willingly, especially if someone else was balking at it. That's the kind of guy he was, likeable and a bit self-deprecating. When volunteering for point, he'd often say, "I'm a dud, and duds never get killed over here."

Ronnie would pipe up and say, "You ain't no dud, Hollenbach. Quit saying that. You're a good soldier."

Each weekday, about 20 or so Vietnamese children would pass by the bunker on their way across the bridge and to school. Hollenbach happily gave them a canteen cup full of wholesome milk, sending them off smiling to school with a full belly. Helping these children was like a personal mission for him.

The Viet Cong hated schools because like Communists everywhere, they wanted to control what people learn. For that reason, they would try to kill teachers, destroy school buildings, or both. It took guts to be a teacher because you always knew Charlie was out to get you.

One morning, Bill and about seven other guys were gathered at one end of the bridge, watching two distant figures walk from the north down Highway 1. As the pair came closer, they recognized the two as an Army Major and an enlisted man with him. As the pair came closer still, they saw it was the battalion Catholic chaplain, Father Hagen, and his Spec. 4 assistant.

If you imagined a stocky Irish priest, about five feet nine inches tall, with short, sandy hair, a healthy ruddy complexion, and an Irish lilt to his speech, you'd be picturing Father Hagen. He was truly a man of God, a priest to all soldiers, regardless of their faith, or lack thereof. Unlike other chaplains who came, performed a service, sang a song or two and left, Father Hagen got in there with the troops. He was considered a direct connection to God.

Although stationed at relatively safe Base Camp in Duc Pho, Father Hagen often ventured into the field to minister to the troops. This day, he had come to inquire about any spiritual needs they had. Sometimes, a soldier might have a pregnant wife at home about to deliver, or maybe he hadn't heard from his wife, or maybe he had a dying parent, whatever. Father Hagen could help contact the family to find out what was going on. Soldiers had enough worries about getting killed or maimed. Worries for what was going on back home only compounded the stress.

Father Hagen ministered to all, Catholic, Protestant, and Jew. To the Protestants he'd say, "We all serve the same savior." On this morning, Father Hagen asked that the small group gathered there join him in prayer.

One hesitant soldier, William Harff, said, "Father, I'm Jewish."

Father Hagen looked at him and said, "That's okay, my son. We Christians are just radical Jews. Come join us."

As the soldiers formed a small semi-circle, arm-in-arm over one another's shoulder, heads bowed, Father Hagen then prayed, "Heavenly Father, bless these men. Provide them safety and protection as they serve their country. Be with them and their families. Preserve their safety and health as they serve their country, and bring them home safely."

After the prayer, Father Hagen announced his intention to visit as many troops on the bridges as he could. The next bridge was a couple of klicks or so to the south, and the good priest decided to walk there.

"That's not a good idea, Father," said Hollenbach. "Sometimes the engineers don't find all the mines, and besides, some Viet Cong could take a pot shot at you. Let's radio for a vehicle for you. We can get the MPs to take you down there."

His assistant chaplain, a little guy about 120 pounds carrying a canvas bag full of Catholic prayer books and New Testaments, said "Father, we need to listen to them. They live out here and they know what's going on."

Father Hagen looked at the sky, lifted his hand and said, "It's a beautiful day in God's world, my son. Let's take a walk down the road, and enjoy the sunshine and all of God's blessings around us. God will take care of us. Have faith, my son. "

As the pair was getting set to leave, the squad members thanked Father Hagen for his visit, and expressed their appreciation for his prayers. Father Hagen said, "God bless you, my boys." The pair then turned and headed down the road, the faithful Padre and his "happy" helper who looked back skeptically at the squad with the face of an insecure puppy that desperately wanted to be somewhere else.

One day Bill received a letter from Susie Wierengo, a high-school friend from Belle Glade, the neighboring town to Bill's hometown of Pahokee. Susie was now a student at Florida State University, where she was the philanthropy chair at Alpha Omicron Pi sorority. In her letter, Susie told Bill she thought it would be a good idea if her AOPi chapter adopted Bill's platoon as pen pals. The idea was the young ladies could write to the guys, and send care packages of goodies, which might make life easier for lonely soldiers far from home. Bill liked the idea. So did most guys in the platoon. He sent Susie a list of names and addresses of more than 20 men who wanted to participate. The way it worked was one girl would write to one soldier. As it turned out, Robyn Ann Green, FSU AOPi member from Dothan, Alabama became Bill's own pen pal. Although Bill and Robyn Ann had never met in person, she became a loyal correspondent who wrote to him about once a week. As the year went on, getting letters and goodies from the AOPi girls did help to make life better for soldiers in the field. It made mail call more exciting. Besides letters, the sorority sisters often sent care packages containing chewing gum, razors, toilet paper, film, and other sought-after items. A group of concerned young ladies thousands of miles away were doing their part in the war effort.

Receiving monthly beer rations was something soldiers, especially soldiers in the field, looked forward to. For some reason, Second Platoon had not been receiving their allotted supply of beer. Were the REMFs taking it? No one knew. All they knew was they weren't getting what they were supposed to get.

That problem was temporarily resolved one day. Bill was walking south down Highway 1 on his way to fill canteens at the potable water station, about a klick away. A slow-moving south-bound convoy of about 20 trucks came by Bill as he walked. In the back of the trucks were pallets of food, and lo and behold, Budweiser beer! The troops never got Bud. Instead, whenever they managed to receive beer, it was usually some off-brand. This beer, no doubt, was meant for officers.

Bill, momentarily overcome by the injustice of it all, decided to take matters into his own hands. He stepped behind one of the trucks, climbed aboard, and using his Buck knife, cut through the cardboard casing holding the beer. He began throwing beer out of the back of the truck and onto the roadside. Cutting into at least a couple of cases, he managed to throw out dozens of beers before hopping off the truck.

The driver behind said "Hey, you can't do that."

"I'm just getting what we're supposed to have," said Bill.

Bill went back to the bunker, and told Don Hollenbach, Iver Brustad, and Ronnie Williams what he had done. Taking empty sandbags, the four of them gathered the appropriated beers, the only Budweiser Bill ever saw in Vietnam.

They decided to have a party and invite some of the villagers to join them. One of the invitees was an old Papa-san who was always hanging around the bunker. Papa-san brought ice from the ville. The guys dug a hole, and filled it with the ice and the beer. About 16 villagers came, and brought bananas and coconuts. They had a great afternoon party. The villagers and the soldiers enjoyed themselves and one another's company. No one fired a shot that day, but the hearts and minds of some villagers likely were won over.

Several weeks into bridge guard, word came that a typhoon was on the way. The squad would have to ride out the storm in their sandbag bunker. To make the bunker more weatherproof, Army engineers had come by and lined the roof with plastic sheeting, beefing it up here and there. Their bunker was probably as secure as anything back at the Duc Pho base camp. Besides, going back to Duc Pho was out of the question. Somebody needed to guard the bridge, storm or no storm.

The day the typhoon arrived, it started clouding over about mid-day. As the day dragged on, the clouds got darker, lower, and heavier, with a definite ominous feel.

The squad was warned to be on the lookout for any ambitious VC who might use the storm as an opportunity to sneak up on them, and toss an explosive into the bunker.

Between thoughts of a tropical typhoon and the Viet Cong, the squad anxiously awaited what was to come. As dusk approached, the rains and wind began. There wasn't much to do but seek the relative safety of the sandbag bunker, and hope the Viet Cong were themselves somewhere tucked in against the weather. Bill knew the Viet Cong were generally civilian soldiers of opportunity, and not hard-core special-forces types likely to brave wind and rain with the express purpose of sneaking up on and killing a small group of Americans.

During the night, the wind howled and rain came down with great force. The bunker's plastic-lined roof began to leak, and everybody inside donned a poncho to prevent getting wet from the overhead dripping. It was a long night, to say the least.

Finally, daybreak came. By then the winds and the rain had let up. Venturing out of the bunker, they saw the water had risen to the point that the only visible dry land was the highway, which now looked like a narrow ribbon surrounded by a huge lake. As they peered into the waters on either side of the bridge, they noticed hundreds of little ripples. A closer inspection showed the ripples were made by swimming snakes, each intent on making it to the highway. Looking up and down the highway, Bill and the others saw that it was littered with hundreds of brown snakes about two feet long. They reminded Bill of garter snakes he had seen back home. Scattered here and there among the brown snakes were a few brightly colored metallic green snakes, the deadly bamboo vipers. Fortunately, their bright green color, great camouflage for bamboo thickets, made them stand out like neon ropes on the highway.

Give guys weapons and put them in the middle of a bunch of snakes, and they're going to use those weapons. They soon opened fire with M-16s, blasting snakes off the road. Then, they took out the M-60 machine gun and went to work on them, rounds going off and snakes flying everywhere.

With all the commotion, word came over the Prick 25 to stop shooting snakes because it sounded like a huge battle going on. Fortunately, they were able to beat back the snakes before any could get into the bunker.

Sometime before mid-November, they were pulled from bridge guard and sent back to Duc Pho for a few days. They had been in the Highway 1 area for over a month, and during that time had become familiar with the area and some of its people. They had taught farming lessons to the villagers, set up a milk station for the kids, and now, another group who knew nothing at all about the area would take their place. Bill wondered why the Army didn't leave them there the whole time, considering they were already familiar with the surroundings. They could have used their knowledge to win the hearts and minds of the villagers, and help secure it better.

Bunker on bridge guard

Guarding the bridge

Bill on bridge guard, Highway 1

Sergeant Westbrook displays a dead snake after the typhoon

Don Hollenbach gives milk and cookies to school children crossing the bridge

Vietnamese school children

CHAPTER 14. OPERATION CATNIP

"Search and Destroy" was the Army's main mission in Vietnam. The North Vietnamese army was invading the south. The best way to stop them was to find them and kill them. To do that, men were ferried by helicopter from base camps like Duc Pho out to the boonies, and dropped off to spend weeks humping heavy packs through hot and wet tropical jungles.

These search-and-destroy missions were given names, in this case, "Operation Catnip," which started in the first half of November. A fleet of Hueys airlifted Delta Company from its base camp in Duc Pho. Early that morning, they climbed aboard the choppers for the fifteen-minute ride to an area southwest of Duc Pho called the Coastal Highlands. The ten or so helicopters carrying the men of Delta Company looked like a fleet of giant dragon flies in search of mosquitoes. The mission was to intercept and destroy the invading 22nd NVA Regiment, which was working its way south in the attempt to overtake South Vietnam. He didn't know it yet, but this operation was to be Bill's first contact with the NVA.

Up until now, Delta Company had mainly engaged the Viet Cong, South Vietnamese civilian-solider communist irregulars in league with North Vietnam. Terrorizing the population into silence, the VC could hide in plain sight among civilians, so you never knew who among the South Vietnamese you were sent to protect was your friend, and who wanted nothing more than to slit your throat.

As the choppers approached the landing zone, helicopter gunships circled, firing rockets into the dense foliage, later spraying the area with machine gun fire, shredding the bushes to help ensure that anyone who might be down there was not left alive.

Upon landing, the first troops immediately formed a circular perimeter to protect those arriving later. As the second group came in, the first group widened its circle, and the second group formed a smaller circle inside it, creating two circular perimeters, one inside the other. As more groups arrived, this process continued until the protective perimeters created a series of concentric circles around the landing zone. Eventually, the engineers with their heavy equipment came to knock down bushes and trees, build bunkers, and construct a working firebase, which became known as Firebase Tempest.

Once the landing zone was adequately guarded, infantrymen began their search-and-destroy mission. Each company was assigned a certain AO. Some officer in the Tactical Operations Center in Duc Pho had maps to show where everyone was supposed to be. This is how the whole thing was organized.

Companies worked independently of one another, usually breaking into platoon-sized patrols. The 25 to 30 men in each platoon searched their own AO to find the enemy, in hopes of killing him before they themselves got killed. It was hot, dirty, dangerous, nerve-wracking work. The men never really knew what they would find, when and if they found the enemy. Would they find one or two intent on sniping at them? Or would they run up against a group much larger than themselves? It was all a guessing game, except this was no game.

Unlike other wars in which the objective was to gain territory, the goal of this war was to kill more of them than they killed of us. A "war of attrition" they called it. Whoever finally lost more men than they could stand to lose would be the first to quit. Instead of large gatherings of troops along front lines, this war was fought mostly by squads or platoons roaming the country's hot, wet, dense jungles. And Bill's own little band of brothers, Second Platoon of Delta Company, was now doing just that.

Every few days Second Platoon would join for an hour or so with the rest of Delta Company to be resupplied. Choppers would bring in C-rations, and any special orders like maybe a new machine-gun barrel.

Each platoon would then go its separate way back to its own AO, patrolling the jungles during the day, and spending hot, wet nights in the jungle protected only by their own perimeter.

As tough as this assignment was, it had at least had one advantage. Here, the enemy was not some Viet Cong disguised as a civilian, but a regular uniformed soldier, easily identified by his light-brown uniform, web gear, pouches and packs. You didn't have to decide whether or not to shoot him. Everybody out here not wearing your own uniform was a bad guy. Your purpose was to kill him, and his purpose was to kill you.

The men of Second Platoon each day searched the hills looking for any sign of enemy activity. They explored the ridges and draws. Whenever they found a stream or other place that seemed like a good ambush spot, they set up an ambush and waited a few hours. Sometimes they found evidence of the enemy, but not the enemy himself. They found huts with grenades, which they blew up with C-4 plastic explosive. They found the beaten-down brush of enemy bivouac areas. They found latrines with fresh human waste, meaning the NVA had abandoned the area no more than a few hours before. The jungle was obviously loaded with NVA. As a member of Second Platoon, you could only hope you found them before they found you.

After a few days, Second Platoon carried out its first successful ambush. They were strung out at mid-morning along high ground with a good view of about 100 feet of a streambed below. Soon, about five NVA came along. They walked casually, carrying their rifles at sling arms. Second Platoon opened fire. One NVA fell into the stream, another in the bushes, the rest hauled ass. Afterward, one body was found, and two blood trails. Following the blood trails turned up no one else. This was the first time Bill had fired at an enemy soldier. Because of the brutal kill-or-be-killed circumstances of war, there could be no reluctance to shoot the enemy. The only question was, could you hit him?

Each day in the jungle brought monsoon rains, so no one ever stayed dry. Troops were issued ponchos but you couldn't fight effectively covered by a poncho. Instead, rain jackets were used. They kept you dry from the outside, but sweat and condensation on the inside ensured you stayed wet. Being wet all the time was demoralizing. Your clothes mildewed, your body got dirty, and soon you couldn't stand your own stench. The rain made for hard humping, especially in the mountains. The first guys in line hacked through bushes and vines, while the last slipped and slid as the trail's mustard-colored soil turned to slick mud, churned by the boots of those ahead.

The 50 or 60 pounds each man carried only made humping that much harder. After a time, a heavy pack starts to eat into your waistline by your hip bones. Soon a raw area forms, then an open wound, which because of the soggy conditions, doesn't heal. Scabs turn soft, then jungle rot sets in. Jungle rot not only tended to attack men at the waistline, but also around the feet. Blisters became infected, then came the rot. The platoon medic would treat these issues as best he could, pouring peroxide on the wound, bandaging it, and telling you to "keep it dry," as if that were possible. Some men got so eaten up with jungle rot, the medic would evacuate them to the rear, so they could "dry out," as they said. After a shower or two, some hot meals, and a few days being dry, they'd be back in the field.

Leeches were a fact of life on Operation Catnip. They were in the streams and in the bushes. They seemed to love to latch on to your neck and hips. Feeling something funny, you'd check and find a few of the little bloodsuckers firmly attached to your skin. To remove them, you'd use your insect repellent, often carried in a two-ounce plastic bottle tucked inside your helmet band. Doused with a few drops of repellant, the leeches would let go. You'd be left with a silver-dollar sized bloody spot with a hole in the center which invited jungle rot.

During the daytime, the men of Second Platoon patrolled the jungle and set up ambushes. At night, they established their perimeter after dark to conceal their position from the enemy. Establishing a perimeter meant setting out Claymores and trip flares, and forming three-man groups around the center. One man was always on guard for an hour, while the other two each wrapped himself in a poncho liner and tried to sleep. The trio sometimes took shelter under a couple of ponchos buttoned together, and staked out to form a hooch.

The nights were long and dark. Staying awake on guard was a challenge. There was nothing for Bill to do but sit quietly, observe the passage of time, and stare from behind his machine gun into the jungle's dark void. As often as not, rain would be dripping off his steel-pot helmet, as he scanned for anything suspicious. Bill knew the rain didn't work to his advantage. Its noise made it hard to hear someone creeping up. Whenever the rain would let up, the wet jungle floor meant there'd likely be no snapping of twigs as the enemy sneaked close in.

At such times, Bill kept his mind occupied and his spirits lifted by singing to himself old red-book Methodist hymns he had learned as a youth. "I Come to the Garden Alone," "'Are Ye Able?' said the Master," and "I Am Resolved." At other times, his mind turned to tender thoughts of the girls he had dated back in the world. He recalled those good times, smelling in his mind's nose their sweet scent, and remembering their soft kisses and caresses. He wondered if he'd ever hold a woman again. But then, his mind would suddenly be aware it was time to change watch. He'd wake his buddy, curl up in his poncho liner, and hope to sleep before it was his turn to guard once more.

Second Platoon's perimeter never was probed at night, probably because the NVA didn't know where they were. Also, the NVA were likely more intent on making their way farther south, and didn't care to engage American forces at this point. Still, you never knew what the long nights would bring.

Food in the field most often meant cold C-rations, the Army's special pre-packaged meal consisting of a plastic spoon, a few cans of food, including a main course, fruit, and dessert. An accompanying accessory pack contained among other things, cigarettes, matches, chewing gum, toilet paper, and instant coffee. These items came efficiently packed in a brown cardboard box about half the size of a shoe box. Each box contained a certain selection of foods. Whenever rations were delivered, the troops took turns choosing what they wanted. The hands-down favorite among almost everyone was Beanie Weenies. Then came chicken and noodles, then ham slices. The last guys to pick usually had to settle for ham and limas, or eggs chopped with ham, these being considered hardly edible.

Normally, you ate C-rations cold, but if you had fuel tablets and the situation permitted, you might use your church-key beer opener to fashion a small stove by making triangular holes in the side of a C-ration can. A burning fuel tablet inside the can provided a heat source, and the can itself provided a place to set your canteen cup which contained the food or beverage you wanted to heat.

Restocking with food had its pluses and minuses. On the plus side, you knew you had plenty of food with you. On the minus side, you had to carry the extra weight.

After days of no enemy contact, word came that the NVA were moving along a certain streambed. Each platoon was ordered to set up ambushes along that stream, about 100 meters apart. At this time, Lieutenant Terry Bender was leader of one of Delta Company's other platoons. Second platoon sat quietly in position along the creek, when all hell broke loose upstream. Sounds of M-16s, bloop guns, and machine guns filled the air. Bender's bunch had successfully ambushed an NVA squad headed south, killing several enemy troops in the process.

While working their way south, the NVA spread out into small groups across the countryside, making them less vulnerable to air strikes than larger groups. Apparently, these small groups had no contact with others behind because those coming later, walked right into the same ambushes. There were several ambushes that day, with four confirmed NVA kills, along with one captured prisoner. If body count was how you kept score in this war, Delta Company, suffering no casualties, was this day's hands-down winner.

The morning of 22 November was wet and overcast, just like many other days in the boonies. Second Platoon had been patrolling the ridgelines and spurs looking for NVA, as had the other platoons in Delta Company.

On this day, Hollenbach volunteered to walk point, as he had often done before. Hollenbach was a good guy, and a plenty-brave-enough soldier. Bill secretly wondered if Hollenbach was trying to prove these things to himself by being on point so often when he didn't have to. Hollenbach's father had been an Army lifer, a Sergeant. Maybe this young soldier was trying to live up to his father's expectations. Only Hollenbach himself knew why he did what he did.

Second Platoon had been assigned to walk well-used trails, trails they had traveled the day before. Walking used trails was dangerous because they were likely places to be ambushed. Everybody knew it, and nobody felt good about what they were doing. Going off trail would have made a lot of sense.

With Hollenbach on point about 50 feet in front of the rest of the platoon, they followed a jungle trail along a ridgeline, then ventured out along the crest of a spur which led slightly downhill and then back up to a parallel ridgeline. After walking downhill they had started up to the other ridgeline, when several sharp cracks of an AK-47 rang out. Hollenbach went down. The fire had come from uphill about 30 feet away.

"Medic! Hollenbach's down!" somebody yelled.

"We need help up here for Hollenbach!" Robert Smith yelled as he moved off trail to the right.

"I'm going up there too!" Bill yelled, as he moved off trail to the left.

Ronnie Williams said, "Watch it Boe, that's a hot trail," and then opened up with his M-60 machine gun, laying down a wall of fire up the trail as cover for those going to retrieve Hollenbach. Bill crouched as low as he could, running as fast as he could to retrieve his friend. The sounds of the machine gun and its accompanying tracer fire momentarily reminded Bill of the tracer fire he had crawled under during Basic Training.

Covered by the big gun, Bill and Smith made it to Hollenbach, who had been hit once in the chest. Bill crawled up next to him. Hollenbach, mortally injured, made one last soft sigh, and then died by Bill's side.

There was no time to mourn. Smith grabbed Hollenbach's bloop gun while Bill retrieved the high-explosive rounds from Hollenbach's vest, passing them over to Smith who lobbed them down the trail to silence any further hostile fire.

The NVA had quit firing. The rest of the platoon began creeping up to provide assistance. In a few minutes, eight or nine men gathered around, including the Platoon Leader, a Green Beret Lieutenant. "We gotta get this guy back up to the top of the hill," said the Lieutenant. "Demon 6 (code name for the Company Commander) wants us to bag him up, and get him up hill."

They were cutting saplings to make a poncho litter to carry Hollenbach's body up the hill, when Iver Brustad from California, who had gone up the trail about 20 feet to provide security, suddenly fired a four-round burst from his M-16. A well-equipped NVA soldier coming down the trail seemed to appear out of nowhere. Brustad spotted him and instinctively opened fire, killing him, eliminating the threat. Brustad's quick action likely saved American lives that day.

From the dead NVA, they gathered a rifle, several hand grenades, and other items of military value, leaving the body lying in the trail as they headed up the hill.

One of the troops, a short-timer, took Williams' machine gun, walked up to the dead NVA, and sprayed him with 30 or 40 rounds saying "G-d damned gook. You killed my buddy Hollenbach."

Somebody else put his hand on the man's soldier and said "You can't make him any deader than he already is. Just let it go, man. Let it go."

Having fashioned the litter, the platoon members took turns carrying Hollenboch's body to the hilltop. In the meantime, James Yoder of Knoxville, Tennessee, another Delta Company soldier in a different platoon had also been killed. Reaching the hilltop, they laid Hollenboch's body by Yoder's. The Company Commander, Captain Harold Sells, helmet off, stood there somber and quiet, staring at the bodies.

The Commander then ordered Second Platoon to move off down the trail, and take a break, which they did. Sitting and sipping water, Bill reflected on how all that action and two American deaths took place in only a matter of no more than 20 minutes. "Here one minute, gone the next, the rest of you guys move out." That how things went in this war.

The very next day was Thanksgiving. Delta Company had been patrolling a ridgeline, and about noon, a chopper from Duc Pho landed in a grassy area to distribute a hot meal of turkey and dressing, mashed potatoes, and green beans. You went to the chopper, got your food, and your platoon disappeared into the jungle to eat. Everyone couldn't stay together in the open because a large group would be a perfect target for NVA mortars. It wasn't the peaceful gathering enjoyed back home, but still it was a taste of home in this faraway and alien land. Instead of the family around the table, your brothers in arms sat together on the jungle floor, eating heartily, each thinking his own thoughts. Somebody said, "It's too bad Hollenbach isn't here with us for this Thanksgiving."

A few days later, Second Platoon had divided into squads to patrol the area. Bill's squad had stopped for a break along a grassy ridge. Seated in waist-high grass, they ate C-rations, and talked.

All of a sudden, someone said, "Who are those bastards coming out of the trees over there to the left? Is that the LRRP boys?"

About 50 meters away, the strangers weren't readily distinguishable because they wore ponchos. NVA didn't normally wear ponchos. In fact, nobody usually wore ponchos.

"We don't want to shoot a bunch of Americans," said a short-timer Sergeant with only a week left in his tour. The Sergeant stood up and said "Halt. Who are you guys?"

At that instant, they began to haul ass, some to the tree line behind them, and some to the tree line about 100 meters ahead of where they had been walking.

"It's a bunch of damn gooks," somebody said.

About this time, Ronnie Williams opened up with his machine gun, firing bursts of five or six rounds as he was trained to do. The others fired their M-16s. Bill fired using his M-16 sights, leading the target as he was taught at Tiger Land. He fired, and one went down. The shooting was over in a couple of minutes. Apparently, it had been an NVA squad on the move south because they were walking fast, with no point man, and no flank support. Once the shooting started, they all scattered. After ceasing fire, the squad went immediately to check out the kills. One NVA soldier who had been hit multiple times staggered down the trail, obviously mortally wounded, but not yet dead. Another in the same condition was crawling away.

"Damn, these bastards just won't die," someone said. They opened fire on the two wounded, and hastened their already certain death. The one Bill had apparently hit was gone, but his pack was still there. In it, they found rice balls mixed with fish, obviously NVA field rations, some awful tasting candy, and a blue sweatshirt. A nearby platoon had heard the shooting, and headed to the Second Platoon's position. They followed trails through the grass, but no other NVA were found.

This was Delta Company's last enemy encounter on Operation Catnip. A few days later, after more jungle patrols, choppers from Duc Pho guarded by helicopter gunships picked them up, and took them back to Duc Pho for a stand-down. There, the men got a hot shower, clean clothes, beer and good chow, and watched movies at night shown on the side of a tent. It would be four or five days before their next mission.

Keith Raitz outside hooch on Operation Catnip

A soldier waits in ambush position.

Bill holds a captured AK-47.

CHAPTER 15. SA HUYNH

Bill didn't know it yet, but December was going to be a good month in country. He wouldn't be shot at, and he wouldn't shoot at anyone. Although he was in a war zone, this month the war would mercifully pass by Second Platoon, now assigned to guard the harbor inlet at a small seacoast town called Sa Huynh, pronounced like "Sah Winn." Located about 20 klicks south of Duc Pho, Sa Huynh's inlet is about 75 meters wide and leads to a harbor in the middle of which is a small circular island about 175 meters in diameter. Created by U.S. Engineers, the island served as an Army transportation and supply base, receiving cargo via amphibious vehicles called "Ducks" from freighters offshore. The island was luxurious by infantry standards. There was a mess hall, a beer hall, and screened windows. A dozen or two shipping containers had been converted into barracks, and sandbagged up the sides for security. Bill thought the island would be a great place to spend the war.

Second Platoon, however, would not be on the island. They would be stationed about 300 meters away, on the high-ground peninsula that separated the island from the South China Sea. Here at LZ Charlie Brown, they made sure the Viet Cong did not access the high-ground area, which would have allowed them to mortar and rocket the island at will. At the peninsula's tip, by the inlet, was an observation and listening post manned by four or five guys.

Second Platoon spent the days at Sa Huynh patrolling the peninsula's high ground, looking for VC. They never found any. The locals could access the area, and they did check identification papers, but all in all things were calm. Perhaps the most outstanding part of this duty was being right next to the beautiful South China Sea. It sometimes seemed to Bill as if he had stepped right into the pages of National Geographic.

And what's a beautiful sea for if not for fishing? Having no proper tackle, they used what they had—hand grenades. Grenades were plentiful. The fish were plentiful. Why not? It made perfect sense. What made even more sense was they were able to trade with the locals the fish retrieved for beer. It was a great system. The grenades would sink fast, explode at depth, and fish would float to the surface. Then, there'd always be some local Vietnamese eager to make the swap.

Besides fishing, seas are meant for swimming. And swim they did. After days and nights in rainy jungles, enjoying a saltwater swim in the sunshine was a luxury they hoped wouldn't end. They soon learned, however, to swim on the incoming tide and not the outgoing tide. It seemed the Vietnamese used the outgoing tide for their sewage disposal system, and anyone swimming on the outgoing tide shared the water with chunks of raw sewage. It sometimes seemed as if every good thing in Vietnam had its drawbacks.

About once a week, the guys from the Transportation and Supply unit would invite Second Platoon to enjoy a steak dinner on the island. The Army island dwellers were grateful for what Second Platoon was doing— namely protecting the nearby high ground so the VC couldn't rain down mortars and rockets on them. To show their appreciation, they'd collect most of Second Platoon in their Ducks and ferry them to the island for steaks and beer. Of course, a few guys always had to stay behind so the place wasn't left unguarded.

While at Sa Huynh, Bill and Iver Brustad were called to see Captain Sells at his bunker. When they arrived, they exchanged salutes with the Captain. He then put his hands on his hips and glared at them in seeming anger. "I want you guys to think carefully," he said sternly. "What have you been doing these last few weeks?"

"We've been doing what we're ordered to do. We've been assigned to secure the hill and the harbor," Bill said.

"We're PFCs. We just do we're assigned to do," added Brustad.

"Well, you must be doing it pretty well," said Captain Sells, "because you two have been promoted to Spec. 4. Congratulations." He shook their hands, and said "Now, get back to wherever you came from."

"Yes, sir," they said. They saluted him and left promptly.

Monkeys were a fact of life at Sa Huynh. Weighing 50 or so pounds, they were aggressive and would steal anything not nailed down. It was bad enough you always had to worry about the VC, but the monkeys only made it worse. They'd run by the bunker door and peek in, hoping to grab a morsel of food or other interesting item. A few of the monkeys would have died for sure of acute lead poisoning, but Second Platoon was under orders not to shoot them. The monkeys came and went as they dared, keeping everyone on his toes. No one wanted to be the next victim of monkey business.

December days ticked by without incident, and then came Christmas Eve. At this time, Bill's thoughts—everyone's thoughts—turned to home. Here in Vietnam, they were aliens from another world, strangers to both their enemies and their Vietnamese allies. Most were barely adults, some still were teens. Not too long ago they had been kids themselves, waiting bright-eyed to see what Santa Claus would bring. Yet, now here they were in their sandbagged bunker on LZ Charlie Brown, each sporting an M-16 instead of a shiny new bicycle. This was supposed to be a day of hope, a day of peace on earth and goodwill toward men. But peace, hope, and goodwill seemed about as far away as California, or Florida, or wherever each man was from. For Bill, this was shaping up to be the loneliest night of his life. He was pretty sure the others felt the same.

Still, they were grateful to be on their peninsula by the sea, rather than in the hot, wet, leech-infested jungles where they had lost Hollenbach and Yoder. Here at least, no one had died. In hopes of making the best of things, someone got the idea of making Christmas trees out of bushes, and decorating them with empty C-ration cans, which they did. Belts of M-60 ammo stood in for tinsel, and atop each bush was an angel crudely fashioned from beer cans. It wasn't exactly what they were used to, but it served as a cheerful substitute. Christmas wouldn't go unnoticed on LZ Charlie Brown. Outside the bunker, dirty fatigue socks hung in lieu of stockings by the fireplace. Through forced smiles, men went about the afternoon humming out-of-tune Christmas carols to themselves.

Soon the afternoon sunlight gave way to evening's twilight and then to the total darkness of another Vietnam night. Each man lay quietly in or on top of the bunker, thinking no doubt of life back in the world. Flares from nearby firebases lit up the night sky, casting momentary shadows over the landscape. The sounds of "I Heard the Bells on Christmas Day," came from a small transistor radio receiving the American Forces Vietnam Network (AFVN), which daily broadcasted music for the troops.

The line about "peace on earth, goodwill to men" caused one soldier to say, "Ain't that something. There's no peace here. NVA always trying to kill you."

Somebody else said, "Bet they're eatin' good back home," at which point the conversation turned to turkey, stuffing, mashed potatoes, black-eyed peas, and cornbread.

Someone else piped up "I guess the VC are all in the ville partying tonight."

The South China Sea stretched out to the east and to the way back home, back to the world, such a long way off.

"I wonder who my girlfriend is out with tonight. I wonder what she's doing," said one.

"She's probably at the same party my wife's at…only drunker," came the reply. The dark humor caused muffled laughter, lifting the somber mood a bit.

AFVN radio now played "Rudolph the Red-Nosed Reindeer."

Just then Captain Sells came in over the PRC-25. "What's that dufus Captain want now?" somebody said. "Christmas Eve and he's probably going to saddle us up to chase some VC through the boonies."

The Captain, known as Demon 6 on the radio, ordered them to report immediately to the helipad, some 100 feet away, to unload supplies from a chopper soon to come in. Outside, the men shielded their eyes from the arriving chopper's cloud of dust and dirt. As they were able to focus once again, they saw a big fat guy with a white beard, red suit, and Army jungle boots jump off the chopper.

"It's Santa Claus!" exclaimed one of the grenadiers. Santa carried a huge heavy red bag of goodies.

"Ho. Ho. Ho. Bet you little grunts thought I'd forgotten you this year," said Santa. "Just got delayed by a little ground fire near the DMZ (demilitarized zone). They fired a few SAMs (surface-to-air missiles) at me, but I made it anyway."

The somber mood had evaporated. "Papa-san, it's great to see you," said one as they all cheered. If for only a little while, the war seemed to recede into the distance. Santa Claus had found them on the far side of the world. It was finally Christmas. Santa reached into his bag and pulled out cookies, cold beer, and other goodies, giving each man a decent share. Then Santa led them in song—"Joy to the World," "Silent Night," "Jingle Bells," and "The First Noel." Everyone sang their heart out, tears streaming down some faces.

Then, Santa said there were others on other firebases he had to visit. He climbed back on his chopper, guarded by two door gunners. As it revved up and left the ground, he yelled, "Ho. Ho. Ho. I'll see you all stateside next year." In a few moments, the only evidence of Santa Claus was the blinking light on his chopper.

This is when Bill saw it—the light from a single star shining much brighter than the others. Someone slapped him on the back and said, "Merry Christmas. God bless you."

Bill smiled at him and said, "And Merry Christmas to you, too."

Back in the bunker, they were now joyous, singing songs, drinking beer, telling jokes, and checking out the goodies Santa had so graciously delivered. They told stories of home, of wives and girlfriends, and others, and dreamt about being home next year.

The next week of course was New Year's Eve, which all in all was a pretty good day. Bill had received a couple of cans of Miller High Life in the mail from his brother Robert, which stood in for champagne that night. New Year's fireworks consisted of bursts of tracer rounds fired over the South China Sea. About half a mile down the coast was a Special Forces camp, which illuminated the night sky with parachute flares. The tracer rounds and the flares lasted only a couple of minutes, but it signaled for everyone that 1967 was done. No more men would die in Vietnam in 1967. That year was history.

Bill's mind turned to 1968, and what it would bring. He knew the good duty they had at Sa Huynh wouldn't last. He'd have loved to have spent the whole war here, or in any one place, such as the bridges on Highway 1. Staying in one place meant that soldiers would get to know the area, and the people in it. If you wanted to win the hearts and minds of the South Vietnamese people, it seemed to Bill that you could better do that by getting to know them, their surroundings, and the dangers they faced. As it was, they were moved often from place to place, and never got much of a chance to get familiar with anything in their AO.

Bill's New Year's resolution was to survive, go home, and help others do the same. On this New Year's day, 1968, Bill was optimistic and happy. After all, this was the year he'd be going home. He'd already survived five months. Surely, he could make seven more.

Sa Huynh

Guarding the inlet at Sa Huynh

Checking IDs while on patrol at Sa Huynh

Bill and Warren Conner at Sa Huynh

Christmas morning 1967 on Sa Huynh.
Harff is in the center looking at the camera. Moose Anderson is directly behind Harff.

Bill and Moose Anderson by their Christmas tree at Sa Huynh

CHAPTER 16. OPERATION GRANT

A few days later word came that Delta Company was to participate in Operation Grant, another search-and-destroy mission, this time in the Quang Ngai province. Ducks ferried the men of Second Platoon from their position at Sa Huynh the short distance to the mainland, where they were loaded onto a convoy of trucks, which then headed north along Highway 1. Delta Company's other platoons, which had been guarding bridges along the highway, soon joined the convoy up to Quang Ngai.

After traveling a few hours, the convoy stopped in an open field where Delta Company spent the night, then was loaded the next morning by platoon into choppers. About five or so helicopters picked up Second Platoon and whisked them away. Bill sat in the door with his feet hanging out. Normally, three guys would each ride on one side of the chopper, feet hanging out, and three guys on the other side would do the same. Two other guys would be in the bay in the middle, totaling eight men besides the chopper's crew. As if there weren't enough concerns in a war zone, for those hanging out the door, there was always the risk of sliding out when the aircraft banked. With that thought in mind, Bill clung tightly to whatever he could find.

Flying at probably less than one thousand feet, he looked down and saw dry rice paddies which reflected images much as glass would. He could see the greens and grays of hedgerows and scattered hamlets, with their brown tops of thatched roofs. Off in the distance the shimmering waters of the South China Sea bordered his field of view. He could see a few people moving around, although not many. It was the dry season, and since there wasn't much to do in the fields until the monsoon rains again came, people weren't out as much. Being so close to the ground, Bill knew that they were in range of AK-47s, an unsettling thought.

The constant anxiety aboard these flights always centered on this one question: "Will somebody be shooting at us when we land?" Coming into a hot LZ was the number one concern. Regardless of what they encountered, they'd have to make a quick exit from the chopper. Sometimes the chopper would actually touch down for no more than ten seconds. At other times, it would hover momentarily about six feet off the ground and you'd have to jump. Weighted down with a heavy pack, two bandoliers of M-16 ammo, and machine gun ammo strung over his shoulders, Bill felt like a huge lead fishing sinker. Would he be able to jump with all that heavy gear, and not injure himself in the process? As it turned out, the chopper actually touched down, and the door gunner hurried them away with a frantic, "Get the fuck off." They didn't come in under fire after all, making for an easy exit.

Once on the ground, each soldier's first concern was to clear the chopper blades, which can swing down and decapitate someone underneath them. The instructions were to clear the blades by running 20 or 30 feet to your side of the aircraft, then hit the ground and immediately begin setting up a defensive perimeter for your group. At some point, the Lieutenant would yell for everyone to go to a rally point, where the entire platoon would form a defensive position in case of incoming fire.

Once formed up, Second Platoon moved out toward the coast, passing among rice paddies and small hamlets in their search for the elusive VC. After a few klicks, they established their nighttime perimeter along a hedgerow, which provided decent cover. Instead of a circle, their perimeter was more of an oval shape within the hedgerow. As always, trip flares and Claymores formed the first line of defense.

For the next several days, the platoon made repetitious sweeps through villages and hamlets looking for VC or evidence of VC. They found none. They encountered old people and very young people, but no one of military age. All those of military age had either been drafted by the South Vietnamese Army or forced to serve the Viet Cong. The village inhabitants seemed as intimidated by the Americans as they were of the VC. None spoke English, and probably wanted to be left alone by everyone to carry on with their lives.

One afternoon, the platoon sent Bill's 12-man squad out to set up a night ambush of a well-traveled trail. Coming upon an abandoned school house, Squad Leader Sergeant Keith Raitz ordered a five-man fire team to check the premises. The tattered, foul-smelling, rat-infested old building proved empty of anything that could have aided the VC. Still stuck to the walls were drawings by school-children of water buffaloes and rice paddies. Disconcerting to Sergeant Raitz were children's drawings of American helicopters going down in flames and American soldiers dying at the hands of Viet Cong bayonets.

Raitz ordered his men to sweep around the entire building, looking for trip flares, stored explosives, or anything related to enemy activity. A few minutes later three shots cracked from one hedgerow over. One hit "Hillbilly," a young man from the Tennessee mountains, in the groin area. Raitz contacted the Platoon Leader who called in a medevac chopper. Ten minutes later Hillbilly was whisked out of the field. The platoon never saw him again. Here one minute. Gone the next.

During the sweep in which Hillbilly was shot, a cherry new guy, only two days in the platoon, motioned to get Raitz's attention. He had discovered a chalk board propped in a chair against the wall. A drawing on the board depicted two NVA soldiers, one bayonetting an American, and another shooting at a fleeing American. The artwork was superb, obviously the work of a talented individual, and not some random villager. Underneath the picture was the neatly printed caption "Die GI."

"I've got to get a picture of this," the cherry said. Having grabbed his Kodak Instamatic camera from his ammo can, he began backing away from the sketch, attempting to fit it entirely into his viewfinder. Suddenly, Raitz grabbed the cherry's arm, and jerked him forward. This 20-year-old Squad Leader from Hector, Minnesota had just saved an inexperienced young soldier from tumbling backward into a huge punji pit, a specially dug hole in the ground, covered with thin sticks and leaves to disguise its presence. Into such a hole, the VC placed sharpened bamboo stakes, often covered with fecal material to introduce infection into any wound they created. Some punji pits were just small enough to trap a man's leg. This one, however, was about four feet square and four feet deep. If the young soldier had fallen into it, he would have been impaled for sure, and likely would have suffered a slow and painful death.

The odd thing about this pit was that it was at exactly the right distance away from the picture that one would need to be in order to place it entirely into the viewfinder of a Kodak Instamatic. At that moment, Bill thought, "The VC know us a lot better than we know them. They know that Americans carry Instamatics. They've probably found them on dead GIs. They know someone would likely want to photograph this image. And he'd have to back into their carefully concealed punji pit to do it." But then he figured, "The VC live here. We don't. They get to watch us during the day when we don't know who they are. We don't get to watch them." It seemed VC Psychological Operations were a deadly force to reckon with.

January involved a lot of fruitless patrols. Bill thought "I know they're watching us. But we don't see them. We know they're out there, but we don't know who they are." He remembered going through clusters of thatched huts, seeing people living on the same land their parents and grandparents likely lived on. He was more sympathetic than suspicious of them. He'd see them standing and watching, or busying themselves knocking husks off rice with a large pestle and mortar. There was no evidence they were doing anything other than taking care of gardens and rice paddies. He knew U.S. troops were here theoretically at least, to protect them from the VC, who'd come into the hamlets and villages to interrupt commerce and education. In so doing, the VC would assassinate school teachers, among others. Bill's mother was a school teacher, so the idea of targeting teachers hit close to home. The VC wanted to control the classrooms, and killing teachers was the way they chose to start. "It takes guts to be a teacher here," Bill thought.

Had the VC killed the teacher at the now-abandoned school house where they found the punji pit? Bill didn't know, but the thought unsettled him.

The VC extorted from those they subjugated by terror, a portion of their rice and other crops, which went to feed not only the VC but also NVA troops moving south through the country. Bill knew this was how the NVA could travel so lightly, not burdened with heavy packs and lots of supplies. They'd pick up from the VC much of what they needed along the way.

One afternoon about 1600 or 1700 hours, the platoon had stopped for the night. They had managed to find an open area about 2,000 square feet in size and about five or six feet higher than the contiguous rice paddy. It was big enough and suitable for the entire platoon, with plenty of vegetation for concealment. Settling in for the coming night, they were cleaning weapons and getting ready to eat. Bill had become a machine gunner at Sa Huynh. His M-60 was broken down for cleaning. Suddenly seven VC appeared walking from the right to left along a rice paddy dike no more than 50 meters away. They were exactly what you thought of when you thought of VC—conical hats, black pajamas, and carrying rifles. They walked briskly along the paddy dike.

Upon spotting them, Second Platoon opened fire. Bill had no weapon other than his .45 side arm. He opened fire with that, knowing the likelihood of hitting anyone was remote. Still, he had to do his part. That was the only time in Vietnam he ever used his pistol. During all the fire, a Second Platoon round knocked one VC off the paddy dike.

The rice paddies had no water in them since it was the dry season. The VC took off running through another rice paddy to a series of hedgerows on the far side. Suddenly, Sergeant Raitz jumped up and said, "I'm gonna get 'em." He took off with his M-16 like a beagle after a rabbit, running the half-football-field length across the paddy, over the dike, and into the far paddy. Two shots rang out.

A few minutes later Raitz returned with a guy by the scruff of the neck, saying, "There's another one back there." Raitz not only had a VC prisoner, whom he had found cowering in the vegetation at the edge of the far paddy, he also had captured an SKS rifle and an authentic Thompson sub-machine gun. It didn't have the circular magazine like you see in the movies, but had a straight magazine. Still, it was a Tommy gun. The results of the encounter included two dead VC, and one captured, plus the captured weapons.

Raitz acted heroically that day. He didn't look the part of a war hero. With blonde hair and glasses, he was fairly skinny, weighing in at maybe 155 pounds. If he had been in a different uniform, he would have been indistinguishable from the members of a high-school marching band. Yet, his actions that day proved that inside this slight young man was a true warrior spirit. War can bring out the best and the worst of people. In Raitz's case, it brought out the best.

That night, they tied up the prisoner, and gave him C-rations and cigarettes. The prisoner's demeanor was cocky and he appeared not at all intimidated. He had been put under the watchful eye of "Dak To" a Spec. 4 who had been with Second Platoon only a short time, but had survived the November 1967 battle of Dak To, which up to this date had been the war's worst battle. At about 2000 hours, the prisoner started yelling loudly in Vietnamese. Just then, the clunking sound of a steel pot hitting a head was heard, and the prisoner went quiet. Dak To had hit him on the head to shut him up, so he wouldn't give away their position. Several times during the night, another clunk from Dak To's helmet punctuated the darkness. The next day, at early light, a chopper came to pick up the prisoner. Captain Charles Cosand, who was later to become Delta Company's commander, came along with an ARVN interpreter.

Upon interviewing the 17-year-old prisoner, they learned he had been fighting for the VC for about a year. During that time, he claimed to have killed five Americans, and seemed to have taken great pleasure in so doing. Captain Cosand said, "Well, boys, you did a good job. This boy's a hardcore VC. He's killed several Americans and is proud of it. He's not going to be doing this anymore. You boys won't see him again." Soon after that, Captain Cosand and the interpreter, along with the prisoner, lifted off on the chopper.

One afternoon, while on patrol and going past a few huts, a small movement in the bushes to the right became apparent. Suddenly, a scrawny chicken ran into the open. Warren Conner, a bloop gunner from Glenwood, Georgia, said, "I think I see supper." Dropping his pack, and handing his M-79 to the man behind, Conner took out after the chicken. After a short chase, he grabbed it by the neck, slung it round, killing the bird in the process.

"A Georgia farm boy can always catch a chicken," said Barham, a good-natured, soft-spoken, sandy-haired guy from Tennessee.

"What do you plan on doing with that chicken?" asked Jim Welch, Bill's assistant machine gunner, from Detroit.

"In the South, we eat 'em. I don't know what you do with 'em up north," replied Conner.

"Conner, let's eat that thing for supper," said Raitz.

Conner then stuffed it into his pack like a pair of dirty underwear, and the platoon continued its patrol.

After another hour or so, they came upon a neglected garden, an onion patch. Normally, they would have left a villager's garden alone, but since this one was obviously abandoned, they helped themselves to a few raw onions. Later, after setting up their nighttime perimeter, which almost always involved setting out Claymores and trip flares, Raitz went around to several guys collecting extra heating tablets—round blue tablets about the size of a quarter, which would burn five minutes or so, and were for heating C-rations. Having gathered a few tablets, Raitz and Conner cleaned the chicken, poured canteen water over it, then skewered it with a Bowie knife. Since the Army had not issued them bayonets, some men carried their own Bowie knife which they used mostly to dig fox holes. Raitz and Conner took turns holding the bird over burning heating tablets for maybe fifteen minutes, then set about to eat it. It proved to be half-raw. Some merely sampled it. Some spit it out. One or two actually ate it, consuming the poor skinny chicken so nothing was wasted. This was the only time they lived off the land by eating an animal they killed.

On 11 January, while humping the boonies, the sound of a distant, muffled explosion came from about one-quarter mile away. The Platoon Leader raised his hand, signaling everyone to stop. The men ceased walking and hunched down. Word passed from man to man down the line that one of the other platoons had multiple casualties. Second Platoon might be needed to provide security for medevacs. Soon thereafter, word came that Second Platoon would not be needed.

Later that evening, the news was that someone had hit a bouncing Betty, the name for a type of land mine which when stepped on is propelled about waist high into the air before exploding. Bouncing Bettys were American mines the Viet Cong managed to harvest from ARVN forces. Because these mines were so lethal, American troops especially dreaded the prospect of stepping on one.

On this day, First Platoon Leader Lieutenant Fred Downs had stepped on a bouncing Betty, and lost an arm.

Around mid-day on 18 January, Bill and the rest of his platoon were once again patrolling the Quang Ngai paddies and countryside. The platoon was spread out over about 100 meters, slowly going along the inside of hedgerows with rice paddies on one side. They had been humping since thirty minutes or so after daybreak. It was a day of slow walking, trying to avoid trip wires, and looking for evidence of enemy activity.

Suddenly, from several hundred meters away, as had happened the week before, there was the sound of a muffled explosion. Instinctively, everyone in Second Platoon crouched and looked in the direction of the explosion. To Bill, it sounded like a booby trap, maybe a mine. Hearing that sound always made him uneasy because it immediately reminded him of that September day a few months back when he had stepped on that mine. You never knew how bad the outcome of a mine would be. Some people died from them. In his case, Bill was lucky, sustaining only injuries to his foot.

One thing about booby traps that especially bothered Bill was you couldn't retaliate. When under fire, you can shoot back. But with a booby trap, all you can do is determine the extent of injuries. The whole booby trap issue bothered Bill to no end.

Just then, the platoon Sergeant received word over the Prick 25, and yelled, "One of the platoons has hit a booby trap and they have a wounded man. They may need us to provide security for a DUSTOFF." A few minutes later the Sergeant again yelled, "Boys, we don't need to go anywhere because they don't have a peanut, they have a Kool-Aid."

The Platoon learned that evening the fatality was Second Lieutenant William Ordway, Third Platoon Leader, killed by a Chi-com grenade, which was part of a booby trap.

Combat Assault - Leaving for Operation Grant

Abandoned Vietnamese school house

Conner (left) and Raitz clean their chicken.

Left to right -- Keith Raitz, Warren Conner, Father Hagen, unidentified soldier

LZ Uptight -- A 105 Howitzer crew provides fire support during Operation Grant

LZ Uptight -- Frank Fosberg, Sergeant Archambo, Barham during Operation Grant

CHAPTER 17.
SOUTHWEST OF DA NANG

Toward the end of January, Delta Company was reassigned to a new AO farther north. The new mission would be to contain and isolate an identified North Vietnamese force which occupied a high mountain ridgeline southwest of Da Nang. The purpose of the containment and isolation was to prevent these NVA soldiers from attacking coastal cities such as Da Nang and Chu Lai. The NVA were itching to hit the cities to show the power of their presence in the country. Delta Company's job was to help make sure that didn't happen by keeping them on their mountain.

In the meantime, other U.S. forces harassed the contained and isolated NVA with napalm, bombs, and air attacks. The hope was maybe they'd turn around and head back to Cambodia. Nobody really knew how many NVA troops were on that mountain. It was certain they had 82 mm mortars, but no artillery.

About a klick or two from the NVA, and on lower ground, Delta Company was on the hill of a ridgeline. Their hill was several hundred feet tall and about a hundred meters long. Between Delta Company and the NVA was a big open valley. A weapons platoon joined the Company on the hill, giving the mortar team ample practice lobbing mortars toward the NVA-infested mountain.

Since incoming mortar rounds from the NVA were expected, the men were told to dig deep holes for protection, with a tunnel going off laterally at the bottom of each hole. During a mortar attack, the idea was they could retreat into these side tunnels and protect themselves from explosions and flying shrapnel.

Since they had not been issued entrenching tools or even bayonets, almost everyone was forced to dig with whatever he had. Bill used the Buck hunting knife Mr. Simonson back home had given him. Fortunately, the earth was soft and claylike, with few hard roots or rocks to contend with.

Buck knife in hand, Bill stabbed the dirt repeatedly to loosen it. With the help of his assistant gunner, Jim Welch, using their steel-pot helmets they dug a hole four feet deep and big enough for three men. The next day, they dug the side tunnel that went back several feet. Others were busy digging their own holes and tunnels.

Looking around and seeing holes and dirt mounds everywhere, Bill thought the place looked like some giant prairie-dog village.

In addition to their holes, they dug a trench about eight feet long and four feet deep, covering it with large limbs they scrounged from the jungle. On top of the limbs, they placed layers of sandbags. An entrance at each end of the trench provided easy access in case of attack.

John Sheppard, one of Bill's ammo bearers, would take off his shoes and boots to sleep. One day, Sheppard was lying in his hooch, with only an OD shirt and boxer shorts on. Bill always remembered the incident at Duc Pho in which the drunk soldier, finished with his tour, admonished the new guys to keep their clothes on at all times. "When the rounds start comin' in, you'll get killed looking for your pants and boots," he recalled him saying.

So, Bill passed that in-country wisdom on to Sheppard. "Shep," he said, "we're in Indian country, and there's more Indians than there are us. If they decide to come after us, I'm going to be in my hole fighting while you're looking for your pants and boots, and you're gonna get scalped." Sheppard ignored him, chewing his Copenhagen tobacco, and spitting it out his hooch.

Another American position was about half a mile away. One night, an exchange of gunfire between those guys and the NVA broke out. Red tracers came from the American side, and green tracers from the NVA side. Ricocheting NVA rounds flew all around Bill and Sheppard. Sheppard frantically searched for his boots. Bill said from the trench, "Shep, get your ass in here before you get it shot off."

Shortly afterward, Sheppard stumbled into the trench, cursing because he'd stubbed his toe. "You're lucky you got your hair, buddy," said Bill. "Did you learn anything tonight?" Bill asked. Sheppard always kept his clothes on after that. He would later turn out to be a fine soldier. He had been initiated into the reality of life in the boonies.

From their position across from the NVA, the men of Delta Company would look at the steep and high terrain the NVA occupied. "If we have to attack that hill, it'll be a suicide mission," someone said.

"They won't need Hueys for medevacs. They'll need Chinooks," someone else chimed in.

As it turned out, Delta Company never got in any firefights here. There were rumors of a ceasefire for Tet, the lunar New Year. During Tet, the Vietnamese customarily traveled to their hometowns to celebrate. You might call it a homecoming, of sorts. The military didn't want a ceasefire because they knew the enemy would exploit it. Still, President Lyndon Johnson gave the ceasefire order, and there was calm in the area.

The first night of the ceasefire, the NVA all lit cigarette lighters from their high-ground position. Hundreds of small, flickering lights dotted the mountainside, making the hill appear to be swarming with fireflies. The next morning, a column of NVA brazenly marched into the open valley below, right in front of the Americans, while observers in an American helicopter watched from overhead. The NVA went on their way without opposition. They disappeared into the jungle, obviously headed for the coast.

"Those guys basically just flipped us off," somebody said. Bill thought back on all the fatigue of hole digging, all the anxiety about possibly having to attack the NVA hill, and all the other efforts expended to keep the enemy contained. Now, because of politics, the enemy simply walked out unopposed, getting a free pass to the coast.

Looking at the mountain where the NVA were.

The weapons platoon fires 81 mm mortars at the NVA.

Delta Company's "prairie dogs" dig their own bunkers.

CHAPTER 18.
THE TET OFFENISVE IN
THE QUE SON VALLEY

From AFVN radio, word was out among the troops that the truce had been violated and there was widespread fighting going on throughout the country. The NVA had used the truce as an opportunity to regroup and take up new positions near the cities. Everyone knew their time on this now-peaceful hill was limited because the mission here was over. There were no more NVA to contain.

A day or so later, Lieutenant Hass called a late-afternoon platoon meeting. The men of Second Platoon stood around casually, not in formation, to hear what he had to say. "Gentlemen," he said, "all hell is breaking loose all over the country. They're sending us to the Que Son valley. It's swarming with NVA, and we're going there to fight them."

Bill had been in-country six months now, long enough to have a good sense of the war. "We are in for a world of shit," he thought.

The very next morning, 3 February, about 10 choppers accompanied by helicopter gunships swooped in to pick up Delta Company and ferry them to their next assigned post—a ridgeline about 26 klicks south of Da Nang, which would come to be aptly named "LZ Hardcore." Those gunships weren't there for looks. They were likely to be coming into a hot LZ.

Because he was a machine gunner, Bill had been positioned by his chopper's door, to provide extra fire power for the door gunner if necessary. Seated on the bird's left side, near the end of the 20-minute flight, Bill witnessed a chopper suddenly shudder and start descending. Its blades seemed to be spinning only by the force of wind, instead of by the motor. Bill watched it go down, landing with a big thump and a hard bounce in a rice paddy. Would the guys on board the downed bird live? Or would it blow up in flames, killing everyone as he had seen in the movies? Guys ran out of the chopper—a Blue Ghost gunship—under fire while a single gunship moved in to provide security. After that, a chopper crew which had already unloaded passengers at Hardcore, brought their aircraft in to rescue those stranded in the rice paddy.

Bill's chopper now swung low on the high ridgeline that was the LZ. On the more northerly side of the LZ were numerous villages, and on the southerly side, a large lake. Bill exited his chopper as it hovered low on the ridgeline. He looked around and saw two dead Americans, each covered with a poncho, and at least half a dozen wounded. The somber sight made his heart go heavy, yet sustained fire from the villages afforded no time for grieving. He had to take immediate cover from the rounds zinging past. Everyone ran to seek cover and to take up positions on the opposite side of the ridgeline, away from incoming rounds.

The choppers left after dropping off their men. The firing soon ceased. Later that afternoon, Lieutenant Haas informed Bill that Second Platoon would be covering the east trail along the ridgeline, the most anticipated avenue of approach for the largest group of people. Hass told Bill to take his four-man gun team, and set up his gun down the trail a bit. If the NVA came up that trail, Haas wanted them to be met with a hail of machine-gun fire. So, Bill along with Jim Welch, his assistant gunner, and ammo bearers John "Shep" Sheppard and Lesley Giles, took cover along the trail, with gun ready for whatever they might encounter.

Perimeter security often requires night-time listening posts or LPs as they're called. Setting up an LP involves sending several men outside the perimeter, where they hunker down, and try to detect enemy activity. If they see or hear the enemy, they're supposed to hightail it back to the perimeter, warning every one of the approaching danger. LP duty is dangerous and nerve-wracking, largely because you're way out front, on your own, and away from the relative safety of the perimeter

Charlie Covington, Frankie Legitt, and one other had been assigned to man the nighttime LP, along with Lesley Giles, one of Bill's ammo bearers. Machine-gun team members are not supposed to be assigned LP duty for a number of reasons. First, they must carry not only their own gear, but also heavy, extra ammo for the gun, meaning they deserve some rest at night. Second, they walk either near the front or the back of the platoon, and the enemy wants to take them out first. Their duty is especially dangerous, so they deserve special consideration for the extra chances they take. Finally, they're more needed to help with the machine gun.

"Boe, do I have to go?" asked Giles.

"No," said Bill, "this is total bullshit, but it looks like an order."

"What's gonna happen if the NVA try to get us?" asked Giles.

"We're not going to leave you out there. We're gonna come get you if the shit hits the fan," Bill said most emphatically.

As daylight faded, Squad Leader Sergeant Keith Raitz, gave the order for the men to move out, telling them to go slowly and quietly. The moment was tense as they headed down the trail along the ridgeline. Bill watched as Covington, Legitt, Giles, and the other guy disappeared out of the perimeter and into the black night.

Bill's turn to man the gun was between 0100 and 0200 that night, making it early morning on 4 February. About 10 minutes before the end of his watch, he radioed the LP for a "sitrep," short for situation report. A negative sitrep means everything's okay. "Lima Papa 1. Lima Papa 1," said Bill into the Prick 25's handset. "If your sitrep is negative, break squelch twice." A few seconds later, he heard the two familiar static sounds of the mic being keyed twice, meaning all was well. The LP was to communicate only by keying the mic, since their voices over the radio could give away their position.

Shortly after 0200, as Bill was leaving his watch, all hell broke loose about 50, maybe 80 meters away, in the direction of the listening post. Automatic weapons fire and sudden explosions broke the night's silence for about 30 seconds, after which all returned to quiet. With no continued fight, Bill's first thought was that the LP had been overrun. The whole incident was quick and violent.

Grabbing the Prick 25, he said in a controlled voice "Lima Papa, Lima Papa, are you guys okay?" No response. "Talk to me. Talk to me," Bill pleaded. Nothing but silence came back.

Lieutenant Haas ran up in a hunkered down position from the Platoon CP. "What's going on?" asked Haas.

"The LP's been hit. We don't have radio contact with them, so I don't know what condition they're in," replied Bill.

"What do you reckon we need to do?" asked Haas.

"We gotta go find 'em," said Bill.

Then came a cry from the darkness. "Oh God! Oh Jesus! I'm hit. Somebody come and help me." After that, came loud moaning and groaning.

"I gotta have an M-16. I'm going out there to get him," said Bill. "Don't light me up when I come back." Taking Welch's M-16, Bill ran down the side of the trail. Staying on the trail was too dangerous. About 30 or 40 meters away Bill found severely wounded Covington off the trail about 20 feet. Bill's first response was to quieten him.

"There's North Vietnamese all around us. I'm going to get you back up the hill, but you gotta be quiet," Bill told Covington. Bill then grabbed Covington under the armpits and proceeded to drag him back toward the perimeter. "God help me get him up the hill," he prayed silently as he kept dragging him as best he could. At this point, Bill lost all sense of time. He didn't know if he had been dragging Covington for five minutes or 15 minutes. The whole world at this point for Bill consisted only of himself, Covington, and darkness.

About 50 feet below the perimeter, Bill said in a controlled but firm voice, "I've got a wounded man down here. I need help to get him in the perimeter." Welch scrambled down the hill, and Bill and Welch dragged Covington the rest of the way back to Bill's machine gun.

By this time, quite a few had gathered around. Lieutenant Haas was there, along with Sergeant Raitz, Moose Anderson, Shep Sheppard, Warren Conner, some medics to tend to Covington, and others. As far as anyone knew, they were about to endure a full-blown ground attack. The medics took charge of Covington, examined his wounds, saying he was shot up but stabilized. "We're gonna get him outta here," one of them said. They then whisked Covington away toward the LZ's main command post.

Now they had to go get Giles, Leggit, and the other guy. Bill turned to Hass and said "Lieutenant, we have to recover those boys. I don't know if they're alive, dead, or what."

The eight or so already gathered around volunteered to go. Bill took point with his M-60 machine gun, explaining "If we run into some shit, we gotta have some firepower." They ventured out of the perimeter, spacing themselves about five feet apart. In five or 10 minutes, they got near to where all hell had broken loose. Hearing movement off to their right, somebody said, "Where are you guys?"

Giles answered, "Hey, man we're down here. We wanna get the hell outta here. There's gooks all over the place."

When they got to them, Leggit showed Bill his bloody right hand now missing a trigger finger. "Boe, they shot my finger off," he said.

"The war's over for you," Bill told Legitt, referring to the nature of his wound. "You're goin' back to Texas."

"I'll be happy to get back to Texas," said Legitt.

"We gotta go get Covington," somebody said. "We can hear him on the other side of the ridge."

"We got Covington already. He's back in the perimeter," said Bill.

"Well, then who's that we hear moaning over there?" somebody asked.

"You boys secure the area, get the radio, and find Covington's rifle. Moose and I are going to sneak over there and find out what's going on," said Bill.

Bill and Moose crossed over the top of the ridge where they could hear groans and movement in the brush. They saw two NVAs, one trying to hold up an AK-47. He had it in his hands but couldn't hold it up. These two had been extensively wounded by the grenades thrown from the LP.

"We gotta kill these guys," said Moose, knowing that two enemy soldiers moaning in the brush would only attract the attacking force to come back on top of them.

"Don't shoot that M-14. You'll give away our position," replied Bill.

Moose looked at Bill. "You gotta knife. Give it to me," he said. Bill handed him his Buck knife. Moose stepped into the darkness, straddled each soldier, and within 30 seconds, all was silent. Moose picked up the AK-47, came back over to Bill, and said "Here's your knife back."

They went back over the crest of the ridge to meet the others, who had by now secured the radio, still had the missing boys and their rifles, plus a cache of enemy weapons. Holding a Soviet .30 caliber drum-fed light machine gun, Conner told Bill, "Man, we found all kinda stuff around here." Another arm in the darkness held up another machine gun just like the one Conner had. In addition, they had captured an AK-47, plus a B-40 rocket launcher. Judging from the weapons they carried, the NVA had sent a sizeable force to attack them. Where that force was now was anybody's guess.

Cautiously but briskly the rescuers and the rescued made their way back to the perimeter. Bill's adrenalin was pumping high. In fact, he had been on overload the last 45 minutes or so. Back inside the perimeter, Lieutenant Haas said "You guys did a great job." He then looked at Bill, and said "What can I do for you, Boe? What do you need?"

"I'd like a can of Beanie Weenies," Bill said. "I'm hungry."

"I'll find you one," said Haas.

About five minutes later, somebody delivered to Bill a C-ration can of Beanie Weenies, which he promptly scarfed down. Later, around 0400, back at his machine gun post, looking down the trail toward where the LP had been, Bill, now off duty, dozed off. He had learned to sleep whenever he had a chance.

The coming daylight woke Bill sometime around 0630. After Welch and Sheppard had retrieved the Claymores and trip flares from the perimeter, Bill prepared his instant coffee over an improvised tin-can stove, fueled by heating tablets. For breakfast, he had a canned bread roll from his C-rations, along with the peanut butter and jelly that came in little olive-drab packets included in his C-ration box. His only other breakfast choice was the C-ration version of ham-and-eggs, which most troops found intolerable. Given his selection, Bill elected to be done with what he had eaten, and move on. Besides, only a few hours earlier he'd had that can of Beanie Weenies.

As they were sitting in their foxholes eating breakfast before the day's tasks began, Giles held up his poncho liner, shot full of holes from the LP firefight. "I'm glad I wasn't in that thing when they shot it," he said. "You guys would be bagging me up to send me home. I'm taking this thing home for a souvenir."

Soon after breakfast, Lieutenant Haas came up and said "You boys had a busy time last night, but we got work to do today. We're going to patrol down to where the listening post was hit last night. We're going to examine the area to see if any weapons got left there, and then we're going to continue on down the ridge to see if there's any evidence the enemy's been coming up the hill."

Shortly thereafter, Second Platoon set out as ordered along LZ Hardcore's eastern ridge. They spread out in single file, about five meters apart. The group's leadership included Lieutenant Haas as Platoon Leader, Sergeant First Class Archambo as Platoon Sergeant, and Sergeant Raitz as a Squad Leader. Bill was the drag machine gunner, meaning he and his gun team walked toward the rear of the Platoon, while the other gun team took a position near the front.

Leaving the perimeter, they proceeded toward where the LP had been. Examining the area, they saw the bodies of the two NVA, along with numerous expended brass casings, evidence of the brief, but intense firefight. Rocks where the LP had been were scarred with bullet holes from incoming enemy rounds. Instead of firing their rifles, the four manning the LP had hit the NVA hard with multiple hand grenades. Rifle fire was not in order because muzzle flashes would have given away their position. With grenades going off all around, the NVA probably had no idea they had engaged only four men. Maybe they thought they had stumbled unprepared onto the perimeter, and decided to make a hasty and tactical retreat. The platoon looked for additional weapons left behind, but found none.

Making their way farther down the ridge, the men split into two groups. Each group walked single file, spaced apart, one down the left side of the crest, the other down the right. They purposefully stayed off the ridge's crest itself to avoid silhouetting the platoon against the sky, making themselves easy targets. In Vietnam, you learned to act as both hunter and hunted. After a few hours, they had found nothing, so they returned to the perimeter for the rest of the day.

To fortify the LZ, Chinook helicopters had brought in a Quad-50 machine gun and a 106 millimeter recoilless rifle. The Quad-50 consists of four .50 caliber machine guns affixed on one mount, which allows the big gun to swivel in all directions. All four guns can fire at the same time. In case of a ground attack, the Quad-50 could shred the enemy into bits. The 106 is a breech loaded, single-shot rifle, about 11 feet long, and weighing over 450 pounds. Sitting on its own tripod, the 106 fires deadly-accurate high-explosive rounds, which can be zeroed in by use of spotter tracer rounds fired from a much smaller .50 caliber barrel attached to the big gun. Once the spotter round hits where the shooter wants it to go, the high-explosive round is fired without changing the aim. This added weaponry made the LZ a more secure home base for field operations into the surrounding territory.

Bill spent the night by his M-60 machine gun, wrapped in his poncho liner. He shared watch with Sheppard, Welch, and Giles. They'd take turns standing watch for an hour while the others slept. So went nights in the boonies. A full night's sleep was unheard of. At first light, watches were over, and everyone was on full alert, all day. Daybreak's first task was always to retrieve the Claymores and trip flares. The mines were placed only at night, when the enemy couldn't see them. In broad daylight, the danger was that some dink could slip up and grab a Claymore, possibly spelling big trouble.

As daybreak came on, Bill threw off the poncho liner, stood up, walked a few feet away, and enjoyed the pleasant relief of a long morning piss on one of Vietnam's bushes. He then went to his rucksack to retrieve breakfast. Opening a flimsy brown C-ration box, he dug out a can of bread, a packet of jam, and some instant coffee. After heating his coffee on his tin-can stove, he used his tiny can opener, called a P-38, to cut into the can of bread. He had just wolfed down the coffee, bread, and jam when Lieutenant Haas walked up. "Here it comes," Bill thought. "Now what?"

Haas summoned the Platoon to come stand around. Outlining the day's plan, he said there was a lot of enemy activity in the villages about half a klick out. The plan was for artillery barrages to soften up the villages. After that, the plan was to move in and mop up what's left. This was not the usual "Search and Destroy" mission. They already knew where the enemy was. This mission's only purpose was to destroy them.

Having received the day's orders, Bill's Second Platoon, along with the rest of Delta Company walked properly spaced and single file down the hill toward the villages. The trail was rocky, with small bushes but no jungle. Within 20 minutes, the entire Company was gathered at the base of the hill, near a no-longer-used railroad track that ran parallel to the ridgeline from which they had just come. A small gulley with an embankment behind the rail bed provided good cover while they waited for the artillery barrages to hit the villages.

After about 15 minutes, they heard the distinct screeching sound of incoming artillery rounds. You only hear that sound if a round is coming straight at you. It all happened so fast there was no time to be scared. Suddenly, two rounds exploded among the troops about 100 feet to Bill's left. He smelled the burning powder, heard shrieking shrapnel flying in all directions, followed by the screams of numerous wounded men. Shouts of "Medic! Medic!" came from all over. Those not wounded began immediately to aid those who were. Captain Cosand, now Delta Company Commander, was himself wounded in the face but maintained command, calling in medevacs to pick up the casualties.

As it turned out, the two incoming rounds were the result of an artillery screw-up. Someone had miscalculated where the rounds needed to fall, bringing friendly fire into Delta Company's ranks. The art and science of war is far from perfect. A computational error somewhere can put you on the receiving end of an incoming round. An artillery round makes no distinction between friendlies and enemy. It simply goes where it's aimed, and does what it's designed to do.

Only a few minutes later, two DUSTOFFs arrived, and somebody popped smoke to guide them in, one after the other. Besides identifying where the troops were, the colored smoke showed for approach purposes which way the wind was blowing, and a soldier in the open guided the aircraft in, holding his M-16 over his head, stock in one hand, barrel in the other. The DUSTOFF pilot would fly straight to that soldier.

The wounded were loaded aboard the DUSTOFFs, and within 20 minutes of the tragic incident, were on their way to definitive medical care. Nine soldiers were injured that day, including Captain Cosand and a Lieutenant whose arm was blown off.

Lieutenant Haas had gotten word over the Prick 25 that the mission had been cancelled. "We're not going to assault the villages. We lost part of a platoon, so we're going back up the hill," he told the men. The demoralized climb back up the hill carrying heavy packs was harder than the walk down earlier that morning.

Back on the LZ, Bill went to look at the new weapons brought in. He had never been on a Firebase which had a Quad-50 or a recoilless rifle. The presence of that heavy ordnance made him feel safer from a possible NVA attack.

The NVA never did try to take the hill, but owning LZ Hardcore was not their objective. They wanted to get into the populated centers like Da Nang and Chu Lai, about 25 klicks and 75 klicks away respectively. Bill knew this was the NVA's all-out offensive. He and half a million other U.S. troops were there to stop it.

The next day, they left the LZ at first light with full rucks to finish what they had set out to do the day prior, before the artillery screw-up.

They had just crossed the rail bed running parallel to the ridge, and at the base of it. They proceeded forward into an open area. Suddenly, they started taking fire. Bill hit the dirt, as did everyone. As he lay there he thought "This is really exciting. I just had breakfast and 30 minutes later, rounds are popping over my head. It's going to be a long month." Bill didn't have a solid grasp of the battle's plan. Why, for example, was he lying in this particular field on this particular day, trying to keep from getting shot? Why were they doing what they were doing, instead of doing something else? The average grunt soldier has no clue of the big plan. That's drawn up somewhere in a bunker, dimly lit by generator-powered electric lights, and staffed with senior officers who make marks on large maps with grease pencils. They decide who's going where and why. The average soldier's plan is to do what he's told, survive, and take care of those around him.

They had been under fire for maybe 60 seconds when the firing ceased. Not being able to find a target to return fire to, they moved to a cluster of nearby buildings. The rest of the morning, there was scattered rifle fire, but no confirmed enemy kills, and no friendlies were killed or wounded.

That afternoon they patrolled the abandoned villages. At one point, sporadic, waist-high rifle fire came from multiple directions. Bill dived behind a huge, waist-high ant hill. Lying there, it dawned on him that an ant hill is nothing but loose, soft sand. It's not going to stop a bullet. He knew he had to find better cover. He stumbled over to a low brick wall that encircled a cemetery. Nearby was a circular burial mound consisting of good, solid dirt. He set up his machine gun facing the incoming fire. The irony of trying protect himself from death in a graveyard went through Bill's mind. "If I get shot, they can just bury me right here," he thought. Then, he identified rifle fire as coming from about 50 meters in front. Although he couldn't see the target, he fired a burst of six rounds as they had taught him at Tiger Land. There was no return fire.

Then, one of the Sergeants yelled it was time to move out. They continued patrolling through rice paddies and villages, looking to engage the NVA, which were swarming in the area, just not where they were.

A few hours later, they came to a river about 50 meters wide. On its opposite side was a thick strand of tall bamboo, a perfect hiding place for anyone with a machine gun. Delta Company had been out all day. The troops were running low on water. The only place to fill canteens was from the river. About 30 meters of low grass was on Bill's side of the river. To get water, he and everyone else would have to go into that open area, exposing themselves to possible machine-gun fire. They were ordered to go in groups of two or three, so as to avoid the possibility of a lot of men being killed at once. Even a poor marksman could have wreaked havoc on them under these circumstances.

Bill and two others ran through the grass, then lay on their stomachs by the water's edge. The water was fairly clear and clean, unlike the water they had gotten before from wells and rice paddies. Bill hurriedly filled his four canteens, then ran back to the perimeter, which had been set up for the night.

Once out of the riverside's danger, he put an iodine tablet in each canteen. Every soldier carried these tablets to purify his drinking water. On an LZ or at base camp, potable water was available in big bladders or tanks. In the boonies, however, a soldier got water wherever he could.

The tablets worked fairly well, but almost everyone got diarrhea their first few weeks in the field. Anyone who had to relieve himself while on patrol, would drop out of ranks for a while, letting others walk by. Later, he would run back up to his place in line.

The iodine made water taste terrible, so the troops learned to counteract the bad taste by adding Kool-Aid powder to each canteen. Kool-Aid was in great demand among the troops in the field. The Army didn't issue it, but relatives back in the world soon learned of the need for Kool-Aid, so it often came in care packages from home. Bill's mother sent him Kool-Aid, as did Robyn Ann Green, his FSU AOPi pen pal. These treats made a huge difference in his quality of life.

Delta Company bivouacked that night near the river. The whole company wasn't bunched up, but separated some distance from one another by platoons. Bill set up his machine gun pointing toward the water, knowing the dinks might try to cross it during the night. The gun team—Bill, Shep, Giles, and Welch—spent an uneventful night taking one-hour turns on watch. Before settling in for the evening, they had put out a good barrier of Claymores and trips between them and the river. No trip flares went off. All was quiet on their perimeter.

The next day, the men ate their usual C-ration breakfast. Eating more than you felt like in the morning made sense because you never knew when you'd have the chance to eat again. C-rations were re-supplied every three or four days. The good feeling of having extra food in your pack was offset by the additional weight you had to carry.

Abandoning their night-time perimeter, Delta Company moved out by platoons in search of the NVA. Although each platoon was separated from the others, they usually had visual and radio contact with an adjacent platoon. Distant gunfire often erupted during the day, signaling that another company had run into dinks.

Elements of the Second NVA Division were scattered throughout the area, and Delta Company along with the rest of the battalion were prowling around looking for them. On this particular day, Delta Company didn't find the war, and the war didn't find Delta Company. That would change the next day.

That night, Second Platoon established a perimeter in a small open area. Sometime around 0200 Bill awoke to the sounds of two guys to his right, about 50 feet away. He could hear them talking.

"Something's moving around out there," one said.

"What do think it is?" asked the other.

"I don't know. It could be animal. It could be a dink. Let's pop a grenade. We don't want somebody coming right up in our laps tonight."

Lying propped up on his elbow, a mere spectator to this whole incident, Bill heard the grenade go off about 50 feet outside the perimeter. Vegetation between him and the exploding grenade protected him from shrapnel. Nothing moved after that. He immediately went back to sleep. Conditioned as he was to the sights and sounds of combat, a nearby exploding grenade hardly phased him.

On the morning of 9 February, Second Platoon, and indeed all the platoons of Delta Company, went through the usual ritual of retrieving Claymores and trip flares, and eating their C-rations. They would spend much of this day penetrating farther into the Que Son Valley in search of the enemy, which the other units had already found.

About mid-afternoon explosions and automatic weapons fire erupted about two klicks distant, and steadily increased in intensity. Shep was behind Bill carrying the machine gun's ammo. "Somebody's catchin' hell up there," he said.

Word came for Delta Company to halt. The message passed from one man to another that Captain Cosand was talking to Battalion about the situation in the distance. As they waited for Battalion to tell the CO what to do, each man followed the protocol of stepping off the trail, dropping to one knee, one man on one side of the trail and another man on the other, in an alternating fashion up and down the line. In so doing, they formed flank security while waiting.

They remained there about five minutes waiting on word from Battalion. When Lieutenant Haas got word over the Prick 25 what was going on, he said "All hell's breaking loose over there. Bravo Company is being overrun. We're going to help them. Captain Cosand wants slicks to come in and pick us up. We're heading into the big shit now." A bit later word came the slicks weren't coming and Cosand had said to saddle up and hump in. Bravo was fighting for their lives, and Delta was the closest unit to them.

At that point, Delta Company headed toward the fight, lined up single file with the idea of relieving Bravo Company by joining up with them. Second Platoon took the lead. Up front, the first man in the entire Company, was the point man. Next was a rifleman, then a grenadier, and next Bill with his machine gun. Welch, assistant gunner, was right behind Bill, followed by Shep and Giles, ammo bearers. Each man bearing the weight of his heavy pack, a slow jog was as fast as they could go. They proceeded along a trail with rice paddies and huts on both sides, heading straight for the sounds of war.

The reports of mortars, grenades, B-40 rockets, and AK-47s all blended together to form a crescendo of death. It sounded as if the entire North Vietnamese Army had zeroed in on Bravo Company.

Lieutenant Haas, from somewhere behind Bill, yelled to be on the alert. "We're about to tie into Bravo in front. Make sure if you have a target that it's NVA, not Bravo," he commanded. The trail they were on led into a village where all the violence was taking place.

As they approached the village, the point man said "There's a trail up here. We're going to cross it."

Just then, automatic weapons fire opened up in front of the proceeding column, and the point man went down. Instead of tying into Bravo, Delta Company had collided smack into the NVA.

"Medic! Medic!" somebody yelled. The platoon medic ran by Bill on his way to the point man.

"Keep moving! Keep moving!" yelled Lieutenant Haas. As they proceeded, Bill saw the wounded point man, down on his right. Blood oozed from a shot to the head, and from obvious bullet holes in each thigh.

"Boe, get your machine gun out there to cover the trail we're about to cross," said Haas. The dirt cross-trail had a knee-deep gully on either side. Bill steadied his machine gun on a nearby rock fence, pointing it down the trail. About 75 feet down the trail, a soldier stepped out and looked straight at Bill. Welch, whose job it was to feed ammo into the machine gun, was right next to Bill.

"Is that an American or NVA?" Bill asked Welch.

"I don't know. I can't tell," Welch said.

"I'm not shootin' down there if it's Bravo," said Bill.

About that time, Lieutenant Haas came up and said "Anybody you see down that trail is North Vietnamese. We haven't tied into Bravo yet."

Bill opened up with six-to-eight-round bursts, hoping to prevent anyone down that trail from firing back. NVA kept darting across the trail, and Bill kept firing at them. They'd run out on the trail, go up or down it a few feet, then disappear to one side or the other of it. As they'd do so, Bill would fire at them. Welch continued to feed ammo into the M-60, clipping new belts on when needed. The rest of Delta Company began crossing the trail, one man at a time. From behind him, as they crossed, Bill could hear guys say "Give 'em hell, Boe. Give 'em some shit."

Gas from the gun clouded Bill's vision, making it nearly impossible to see where he was firing. "You're shootin' too high," said Welch. "Bring it to the left," he added. "Dammit Boe, you got one." Bill kept firing.

As Captain Cosand came by, he reached down, touched Bill on the shoulder, and said "Keep shootin', buddy. Keep shootin'."

About 50 feet from Bill, Delta Company finally tied into Bravo. As the last platoon passed by Bill, its leader said "We've tied into Bravo. Move on in with us. Bring the machine gun, buddy." Bill had started out in the front of the Company and ended up in the rear. He had fired about 600 rounds down the trail, scoring what would later be one confirmed kill.

Bill was the last man to enter the perimeter. Everything around him was chaos. The first thing he noticed were two Americans kneeling and firing. They were haggard, and looked exhausted. One of them turned to Bill and said "Buddy, we're glad you're here. We've been through a lot of shit."

Other men ran back and forth looking for a place to fight, seeking to establish a perimeter defense against the NVA, which were firing at them from all directions. The area they were in was more or less open, but there were also scattered bushes, hedgerows, and vacant buildings. This was the outer edges of a village decimated by war.

Bill looked to one side and saw a dead NVA. Not long before, the enemy soldier had been a deadly combatant. Now pacified, his motionless body lay there, right arm on his chest, left arm outspread and his right knee cocked over his left. Not far away was another dead NVA, making it obvious that there had been close combat—probably hand-to-hand combat.

Suddenly, incoming mortar rounds caused confusion and panic. There was no place to hide from the shrapnel, much less the explosions. The sounds of nearby NVA mortars going down into their tubes and being launched reminded Bill of the sounds of Fourth of July rockets when they first take off. Unlike screeching artillery rounds, mortars make no noise coming down. There are only two ways to escape a mortar—either get in a hole, or run. Guys were running from the impact area, darting around looking for ground cover. There was none. Some low-crawled, looking for protection. Confusion bordered on panic. Besides the mortars, there were the sounds of automatic rifle fire, and sights of numerous shoulder-fired B-40 rockets flying by like red streaks in the air. The rockets would pass shoulder high on their way to deliver their deadly payload.

In the midst of all this, other soldiers were carrying numerous wounded men down a path that led through some foliage. Bill couldn't see where they were going, but at least they seemed to have a plan.

Bill was standing with his pack and machine gun, looking for protective cover. He had been separated from Delta Company back when he was firing down the trail. Now, he couldn't find his platoon. Everyone was trying to shield himself from incoming rounds. The dinks were firing from everywhere.

Then he saw Barham, a grenadier from Delta's Second Platoon, running by about 15 feet away. While Bill was watching, a bullet slammed into Barham's head. It sounded like a hammer hitting a piece of metal. Barham spun around, and collapsed on the ground.

Then Captain Cosand literally walked up, standing erect in spite of bullets and shrapnel flying everywhere. "You guys gotta get organized, get down, and start fighting," he commanded. Seeing a man squatted, Cosand looked squarely at him and said "Dig! Dig a hole. Dig here." "You dig there," he told another. "We got some fighting to do." In the heat of horrendous battle, this infantry officer, who had been wounded in the face the day of the artillery screw-up and still wore his bandages, calmly walked around helping bring fighting order out of battlefield confusion, by telling his men exactly what to do. Captain Cosand's courageous action in spite of the danger all around him was one of the most heroic things Bill would experience during the entire war.

From about 30 feet away, Bill heard a familiar voice. Ronnie Williams, who used to be machine gunner, and now lead the weapons squad, called to him.

"Boe, come over here. I'm diggin' in. Get in the hole with me." Bill scrambled over to where Ronnie was. Together, they dug like mad, using Bill's Buck knife and their steel-pot helmets. Fortunately, the soil was fairly soft. In five minutes or so, they had scraped out a trench about five feet long and 18 inches deep. They had a life-or-death need to move dirt, and that's what they did.

Next to them was John Gentry, from the Show-Me state, rapidly throwing dirt between his legs in a desperate attempt to go subterranean as fast as possible. "Looks like a Missouri blue-tick hound over there digging for a bone," Bill thought, using his self-protective sense of humor to create a bit of levity in this hellacious scenario, even if the levity was only in his own mind. Mortars were still slamming in from everywhere.

Bill knew his and Ronnie's hole wouldn't protect them from a direct hit, but it would at least shield them from flying shrapnel. They continued to dig deeper, knowing their hole had to be a good fighting position, and they didn't know how long they would have to remain here and fight.

The other members of Bill's gun team—Welch, Shep, and Giles—had blended in somewhere else. From their hole, Ronnie and Bill heard from about 200 feet away, across the now-established perimeter an eruption of intense automatic weapons fire. Within a few minutes, the intense firing diminished. Bill figured the NVA had tried to overrun the perimeter but were beaten back.

The news of what had happened began to pass by word of mouth from hole to hole. Bravo Company had made an unsuccessful attempt to punch through the NVA encirclement to create a corridor through which to withdraw to LZ Hardcore. Bravo and Delta Companies needed to abandon the area so artillery and air strikes could annihilate the concentrated contingent of NVA. That was the plan, but that plan had failed. There was no getting out. They'd be staying here tonight to fight it out against an enemy force which had them surrounded and massively outnumbered.

The word came via each foxhole that they'd be staying put. Ronnie told Bill "I'm glad we've got that machine gun. It looks like we're in for a fight."

Bill told Ronnie "I gotta machine gun, but I ain't got much ammo to go with it. I fired a bunch of rounds. I've got 200 rounds left."

Ronnie, who was now a buck Sergeant, said "You'd better go find some more. We're going to need more than that."

Bill ran bent over at the waist, checking out abandoned packs and other debris strewn all about, looking for any M-60 ammo he could find. When he'd see some, he'd grab it and run look for more.

Running through a clear spot through the brush, he came up on a bomb crater about waist deep and maybe 15 feet in diameter, with a small berm around it. To Bill it looked like an old B-52 bomb crater. Inside the crater came the cries and groans of about 20 wounded men. Some had IVs in their arms thanks to the medics who were tending to them.

Still searching for ammo, Bill ran right by Captain Cosand, who likely noticed Bill was running and had no rifle. The only weapon Bill had at the moment was the .45 semi-auto pistol strapped to his hip.

Cosand yelled to Bill "Where are you going, soldier? You need to be back there fighting."

"Captain, I'm an M-60 machine gunner who's already fired over 600 rounds today when we tied into Bravo Company. I don't have much ammo left, and I need to find some."

Cosand's demeanor changed from confrontational to supportive. "You better find as much as you can because we're going to be in for a hell of a fight," he said.

About this time, Bill heard a guy on a Prick 25 seated on the berm around the bomb crater say "Boys, medevac's coming in. Pop smoke." Bill heard the click of a smoke canister's pin being pulled. Then he saw purple smoke rising to the left of the crater. Just then, a chopper approached nose down and low at a height of about 50 feet, barely clearing the foliage. Its powerful rotors churned up dust and purple smoke. Bandages and other debris littering the ground were blown in all directions. A hail of green tracer rounds came at the chopper from beyond the perimeter. As the mercy bird painted with big red crosses on a white background settled in next to the crater, people began hurriedly picking up, carrying, and loading the bloodied, and in some cases, unconscious wounded onto it. Medics dragged as many as they could as fast as they could. Casualties packed the chopper. There was even one in the door gunner's seat. Bill thought that if the door gunner's seat on the other side also had a casualty, this was essentially an unarmed chopper. Within three minutes or less of landing, the chopper's engine revved, lifting it about 20 feet in the air and it went out in the opposite direction from which it had come, tail up, nose down, its skids barely clearing the bamboo in its path, taking massive amounts of enemy fire.

"Another bird's coming in. Get those guys ready," somebody yelled, and a plume of green smoke went up to mark the landing zone. Bill heard engine sounds of the approaching chopper, accompanied by a crescendo of automatic weapons fire. A flurry of green tracers attacked the incoming aircraft, making pinging metallic sounds as they penetrated its skin. Since only each fifth round was a tracer, the number of bullets hitting the aircraft was much more than the sights of tracers indicated. As the chopper came in low and fast, Bill saw the intense look on the pilots' faces. He heard them slow their engine speed, then suddenly accelerate and keep going over the trees, aborting their landing.

Somebody on a Prick 25 announced "They're being chewed up by incoming fire. Not coming in." Then someone who was likely a Lieutenant, but without insignia Bill didn't know for sure, said to those around him "No more choppers coming in. We'll take care of the wounded as best we can."

With the ammo he had picked up here and there, Bill returned to his and Ronnie's fighting position. Guys were still digging in, attempting to make their raggedy, hastily dug holes as protective as possible. Ronnie and Bill dug some more, too. After an hour or so, their hole was waist deep and marginally comfortable. They wouldn't be able to stretch out and sleep in it if they needed to, but at least they could now take good cover from incoming rounds and shrapnel.

As dusk settled in, Bill and Ronnie ate a C-ration meal and talked of what they would do if they got of this place alive. Ronnie said "I need to take Betty and go to Galveston. We're going on some trips. What are you gonna do, Boe?"

Bill thought a moment, and said "All my life I've been using somebody else's car. My brother would let me use his '64 Catalina. I'm 21 years old. I need my own car."

"Get something fancy," Ronnie said. "Get a Pontiac GTO."

"I don't need a GTO," said Bill.

"Need it, hell, just get it," said Ronnie.

Then, from one of the holes flanking his position, Bill recognized a familiar voice. "Barham! Is that you?" asked Bill. "Good God. I thought you were dead, shot in the head."

"I thought I was dead too," said Barham. "I had a bullet slam into my helmet. I pulled it off and there was no blood, just a hole in my helmet. The bullet just ran around inside my helmet liner. I'm keepin' this thing for a souvenir. I'm not turning it in." For the rest of his tour, Barham proudly wore that helmet, which had a hole in it between where the forehead and the right ear would fit. It was a conversation piece almost every time someone new saw it.

Once more, mortar rounds began to drop inside the perimeter, hitting about 100 feet or so behind Bill and Ronnie's hole.

A bit later, shortly after dark, more weapons fire started coming in. A steady stream of green tracers whizzed by about two feet above their hole, reminding Bill of the infiltration course he had gone through in Basic Training.

"Remember that firepower exhibit they put on for us at Fort Polk?" said Ronnie. "They showed us all what they'd have for us. They said 'We'll bring in the air strikes and artillery. All you got to do is go in afterwards and mop 'em up.' Remember that, Boe? They'd shoot the junk vehicles and say 'Boys, this is what you're going to have. We'll send you in afterwards with your rifles, and you just go clean 'em up.' Where's all that stuff now?"

"I don't know," said Bill. "I don't think it's comin'."

As the tracers kept flying just above them, Ronnie said "You reckon those bullets are going to get us?"

"I don't think so," replied Bill. "Not unless they can make a 90-degree turn down here in our hole. I think if we just keep down, we'll be okay."

After about 2000 hours, the firing diminished. Artillery fire began to hit suspected NVA positions on the other side of the bamboo, not far from where they had dug in. It seemed the artillery had good coordinates and were steadily hitting the near-by NVA positions just outside the perimeter, apparently causing the NVA to back off.

Only 30 feet or so from their foxholes was a thicket of bamboo chewed up by rifle fire and explosions. From this thicket, the enemy fired at them sporadically with AK-47s. The intensity of the incoming fire, however, was much less than they had endured earlier. What they were experiencing now was likely exploratory fire, an enemy attempt to provoke them into firing back, and disclosing their positions. If the dinks knew where they were, they might slither into the perimeter, low-crawling like worms up to each foxhole. To help prevent such an intrusion, guys lobbed grenades throughout the evening into the bamboo thicket. They weren't throwing them at anyone specifically. They did it to keep the dinks away.

After about 0200, all was quiet except for the explosions from the grenades thrown at the bamboo thicket. At first light, men began calling back and forth to those in the next hole. "Gentry, you okay?" said someone.

"Fine. But the dude in here with me stinks," came the reply. Such bantering went back and forth for a while until everyone was satisfied no dinks occupied the foxhole next to them.

Through the foxhole message-relay system came the news that they were going to bring in gas masks and saturate the area with CS gas to drive out the dinks. After that, they were to recover the bodies of their own dead, those killed the night before.

Now broad daylight, two F-4 Phantom jets, probably out of Da Nang, shrieked by low overhead, a couple of hundred feet up. Coming in for a low run, each jet would drop its bomb. A few seconds later, the bomb would find its target, exploding in a huge cloud of fire and black smoke, after which the jet would climb and circle back to make another run. If the dinks were still over there, they were surely catching hell. Bill thought that the airstrikes demonstrated at Tiger Land had finally arrived. Those jets were a most welcomed sight.

Later on that morning, after the Phantoms had made their runs, resupply choppers delivered gas masks, along with more ammo and C-rations.

Bill's Second Platoon, along with a platoon from Bravo Company, were ordered to sweep in front of their respective perimeters to search for continued presence of NVA. Second Platoon found an NVA body down the trail where Bill had fired the 600 rounds with his machine gun. The top of the head was missing, indicating the enemy soldier had been killed by a bullet and not shrapnel. Bill's machine-gun team got credit for the kill. They also found a half-dozen Chi-com grenades, a pineapple grenade, an AK- 47, and two SKS rifles. Bravo Company did a similar sweep and found several dead NVA.

A 105-Howitzer artillery barrage saturated the area beyond the defensive perimeters with CS gas. Unlike the gases used during World War I, CS gas isn't lethal. Bill remembered being introduced to it back in Basic Combat Training—in the "gas house," they called it. With your gas mask firmly in place, they'd usher you individually into a small concrete-block building. Inside, the fog of gas was so thick you could hardly see. Then, some Drill Instructor would order you to remove your mask, say your name, rank, and serial number, after which you'd have to walk—not run—out of the building. The whole idea was to give you a good dose of CS gas so you'd know its effects. CS, essentially a riot gas, disorients a person, making their eyes tear and burn, their throat seem to seize up, and their nose run copiously. Because of its initials, it became known among the troops as "chicken shit" gas. Its purpose here was to disorient enemy troops, render them incapable of fighting, and make them run from the area.

With weapons in hand, and gas masks affixed, Delta's Second Platoon accompanied a platoon from Bravo Company on a mission to find a missing squad, presumed dead from the previous afternoon's fighting. Second Platoon's purpose was to provide security for what was believed to be a body-recovery operation.

CS gas covered the area like a huge, white ground fog. As he walked through the billowing clouds of gas, Bill primarily concentrated on making sure his mask was properly sealed. The mask had two clear panes, one over each eye, to allow the wearer to see ahead. To look left or right, he would have to turn his head. What's more, it was hot inside the mask. Bill struggled to breathe. He carried his heavy machine gun, but at least he didn't have his pack to contend with. They'd been told to leave their packs at their foxholes, their new homes for the time being.

Passing through a hedgerow, they turned to the left, encountering several small, war-torn houses. They'd been out about 10 minutes, and no shots had been fired. Then, a voice off to Bill's left announced "Bodies over here." Eight or 10 men from Bravo Company went over to a small trench, where the bodies were. Bill, part of the security team, observed them from about 50 feet away, machine gun ready.

"Oh my God," said someone. "These guys are all dead."

Bill stood guard as he was supposed to, facing away from the scene, but looking now and then over his shoulder to see what was happening behind him. He saw men reaching into the shallow gulley, grabbing bodies by the legs and arms, pulling them out of the depression. Bill watched as the bodies kept coming. "Good God," Bill thought. "How many people have we lost?" As it turned out, Bravo Company had lost an entire squad—about eight men.

The walk back to the perimeter reminded Bill of a funeral procession. The bodies were carried up front, and Bill with his machine gun helped guard the rear. He felt like the highway patrolman who's always last in line as the funeral cars with their lights on process toward the cemetery. There was no loud talking among the men. Everyone spoke in soft, reverent tones to show respect for their fallen brothers.

Back inside the perimeter, near the command post, bodies were lined up in two rows. Each was lying supine, covered with a poncho, boots sticking out, toes pointing skyward. In addition to the bodies just recovered there were the remains of four men from Delta Company who had died in the last mortar attack the night before. A mortar fell right into their foxhole. That same mortar attack wounded 16 others. After that last DUSTOFF couldn't land due to heavy fire, no more came to evacuate the wounded until daylight.

Bill watched as medics and Lieutenants on their knees went about uncovering the faces of the dead to properly identify them. They'd look at one, write something, then go to another. The gruesome sight of a dozen men lined up dead would always remain in Bill's memory of the war. Later that day, choppers came in to transport the bodies back to LZ Hardcore, to begin the long, flag-draped journey home.

Helicopter gunships circled the perimeter the rest of the day. Nothing eventful happened. As evening approached, they put out Claymores and trip flares in front of their perimeter in case the NVA came back. None did. All was quiet.

The next day, Bravo and Delta Companies humped back to LZ Hardcore, accompanied by helicopter gunships. The two companies, now short on men due to casualties, walked single file, spaced 10 to 15 feet apart. Good spacing always made sense. Snipers liked to shoot at people bunched up. Plus, an incoming mortar round would cause fewer casualties since the men were spread out. NCOs and Officers often reminded the men of good spacing. "Keep your distance," they'd say. Or "Spread it out. Don't bunch up."

The gunships circling overhead reminded Bill of the crop dusters he'd seen growing up in his little south Florida truck-farming community. They'd come in for a run, circle around, and then come in again. Bill felt safe seeing them up there covering point and both flanks. He suspected the gunships could see if there were any NVA in the area.

About half a klick out they could see the ridgeline that was LZ Hardcore. What was behind them was now in the past. Those who had made it through looked forward to a better life once they were back on the distant hill ahead. Arriving at the same ridgeline where they'd landed under fire eight days prior, and where the listening post had been attacked, it now felt like home—a safer and more secure place than the places they'd been.

Crater made by the friendly artillery round

John Gentry in his rapidly dug foxhole after tying in with B Company.

An F-4 Phantom jet provides air support, knocking out NVA positions.

Captain Charles Cosand,
Delta Company Commander during Tet/ Tet counteroffensive.

Captured NVA weaponry after the Tet attack

CHAPTER 19.
RETURN TO LZ HARDCORE

On the LZ once more, everyone returned to the positions they'd occupied earlier. Bill's gun team set up on the east trail as they had done when they first arrived. For the first time in weeks, Hueys brought in mail in the familiar red bags. Bill got letters from his mother, his brother, and Robyn Ann Green. Robyn Ann wrote to him throughout his tour. Her letters often contained chewing gum and other goodies that made life in the boonies more bearable. Everyone in Second Platoon loved receiving letters from the AOPi girls, which often included pictures of them at some social function dressed stylishly, and probably smelling as good as they looked in the photos. Such images reminded everyone that life was still going on back in the world. Bill liked the pictures of Robyn in her FSU tank tops. He wondered if he would ever meet her.

Besides the mail, the Hueys also brought in clean clothes, and once a day, hot chow in large green mermite containers. When it was his turn to exchange clothes, each man would leave his position, and go over towards the CP, and select clean fatigues and underwear from among those laid out on a large tarpaulin spread on the ground. He'd shed his old clothes, leave them there, and don clean ones.

The Army had brought in a water wagon filled with potable water. You could fill your canteen from the wagon's spigots, and drink the water straight, with no need to add iodine. The men finally got a chance to shave, and even wash up a bit, using their steel pot helmets as a basin. The AOPi girls had sent real soap, an added luxury.

Back at their machine gun position, Lieutenant Haas walked up carrying a large envelope. "Welch," he said, "you got something from the Red Cross." Red Cross messages could contain good or bad news. You never knew.

Taking the envelope from Lieutenant Haas, Welch opened it with optimistic expectations. Upon seeing its contents, Welch, broke into a huge grin, flashing his healthy white teeth. "Man, I've lived to be a father," he said. "We've got a baby! Our first child."

The envelope contained three cigars. Welch reserved one for himself, then gave one to Ronnie Williams and one to Bill. They shared the joyous moment as Jim Welch, half a world away from his wife and child, personally lit each cigar. Welch was quite the sight as he proudly puffed away, a handsome young man with a thick shock of black hair, dressed in an unbuttoned fatigue shirt, his dog tags hanging loosely around his neck. Atop this faraway hill from which they could see miles of Vietnamese countryside, the trio celebrated new life in spite of all the death they had encountered.

Things had quietened down on Hardcore, but that didn't mean the war had let up. The NVA were still out there somewhere, and everyone knew it. Checking out the hill's defenses for the second time, Bill wandered over to look once more at the 106 millimeter recoilless rifle. Perched on its tripod in a flat area on the ridgeline's north side, and protected somewhat by a low bank of sandbags, the 106 could hit almost anything in the valley below. Unlike artillery rounds which arced up and then came down, 106 rounds went straight to the target.

Bill stayed back 30 or 40 feet watching the weapons specialist seated at the big rifle. Another soldier stood nearby peering into the valley below with binoculars. A third, most likely an officer, crouched bent at the waist, observing the goings-on.

"We got some gooks down there looking at us," said the guy with the binoculars.

"Can you hit 'em from here?" the observer asked.

"Oh yeah," said the weapons specialist, swiveling the 106's barrel in the direction of his newfound target. "Are they still there?"

"Yeah, they're still looking at us," said the guy with binoculars.

The weapons specialist fired a spotter round, sending a slender orange tail of fire to the valley floor below, about half a klick out.

"That's right on top of them," said the guy with binoculars.

"Hit 'em with an H-E."

"Lookout for the back-blast," the weapons specialist yelled over his shoulder. He then fired a high-explosive round. A red trail of fire led straight to where the spotter round had hit, creating a distant explosion.

"Man you took 'em out. You got 'em," said the guy with the binoculars.

Having seen the 106 in action, Bill went back to tell the other guys what had happened. Along the way, he wondered if the NVA targets had been forward observers for a mortar team planning an attack on Hardcore. If so, the 106 pretty much screwed up their plans.

Bill was impressed by what he had seen. While he humped the boonies with a 40-pound pack and a machine gun, engaging the enemy in grimy close-quarters combat, the guys in the weapons platoon sat up there on a high hill, spotting the distant enemy through binoculars, and firing at them from half a klick out. To Bill, that made a lot of sense. It seemed like a more practical, and efficient way to fight a war.

Jim Welch (center) shares cigars with Ronnie Williams (left)
and Bill to celebrate the birth of his child.

A weapons specialist operates the 106 mm recoilless rifle on LZ Hardcore.

Bill and Warren Conner on LZ Hardcore

CHAPTER 20.
TO THE SOUTH OF HARDCORE

A day or so later, Lieutenant Haas called Second Platoon's Squad Leaders to his CP. Such a meeting usually meant something was up. The Army operates by a strict chain of command. Battalion tells Company Commanders what's going on. Company Commanders tell their Platoon Leaders. Platoon Leaders tell their Squad Leaders. Squad Leaders tell their men. Soon after the meeting with Lieutenant Haas, Sergeant Ronnie Williams, leader of the weapons squad, came by Bill's machine-gun position to fill him in on the upcoming mission.

"This is what's gonna happen," said Williams. "We're leaving here tomorrow to go into that valley south of us and see what we can find. Then we're going to that mountain range on the other side of the valley, to find out what's over there. If there's NVA out there, we're gonna get 'em. Make sure you've got grenades, trip flares, ammo and all the other stuff you'll need. If we run into NVA, our platoons will be together, and we'll bring in firepower to support us."

Grenades, ammo, Claymores, trip flares, smoke canisters, and other military items came as a result of a periodic resupply requisition, called the "grocery list." Squad Leaders would ask each man in his squad what he needed. They'd submit their squad's list to the Platoon Sergeant, who'd then submit a compiled list to the Platoon Leader. More often than not, the requisitioned items would arrive the next day on a resupply chopper.

Each man normally carried two hand grenades, sometimes up to four. Bill figured the M-26 hand grenade was the best weapon they had. Besides its steel casing which broke into shrapnel chunks, the M-26 was loaded with a great length of fine wire, meant for shredding anything or anybody in range of its blast. Grenades were effective for knocking out enemy gun positions, and were essential in nighttime firefights since a rifle's muzzle flash would expose your position. M-26 hand grenades were what saved the boys on the listening post.

Once per month, the resupply chopper would deliver the "sundry packs," boxes filled with goodies such as Hershey Tropical Bars, assorted fruity candies, and cigarettes. The contents of one box was split among the members of one platoon. The Tropical Bars, designed to hold up in Vietnam's heat and humidity, were barely sweet. The joke was that it took three months in country to start liking them.

Before any mission, each man knew to pack adequate C-rations, and to fill his canteens from the water station. They distributed the C-rations equitably. Whoever got first pick last time, got last pick this time. The Beanie Weenies always went first. Several cigarettes came in each box of Cs, and non-smokers sometimes traded them for desirable items such as fruit cocktail, canned pears, or canned peaches.

Many of the men used the evening to write letters back home. Bill often wrote to two particular girls—Robyn Ann Green, and Joanne Harris, a girl from home, four years his junior, still in high school, a little-sister type who wrote to him quite often. He usually shared what he could about upcoming missions. Bill wanted people to know his situation. If he died, he didn't want them unaware of what he had experienced.

The next day, Delta Company left Hardcore, heading south into the valley, an area of active agriculture full of rice paddies, hedgerows, and a few buildings. The platoons made their way adjacent to one another, about 100 meters apart, with the men of each platoon proceeding in single file, spaced about 15 feet apart. The point man for each platoon stayed about 50 feet in front, and a man assigned to rear security stayed a similar distance in back. Sometimes, when the terrain permitted, four men from each platoon guarded the flanks. Two took up positions near the front, one on each side. And two positioned themselves near the rear, one on each side.

The first enemy encounter after leaving Hardcore took place about mid-day on 19 February. Second Platoon was walking slowly in a fallow rice paddy, next to a low dike on the left. Up to this point, there had been no signs of NVA in the valley. Everyone was beginning to suspect that the dinks were in the mountains ahead. Now and then, at the base of those mountains, the men would hear sporadic rifle fire, and the pounding sound of an occasional artillery round hitting somewhere up in the hills.

Their mission right now was to search the valley and destroy any enemy troops found there. They patrolled slowly, in no hurry to get to the mountains, especially since things in the valley had been non-eventful. Occasionally, they'd stop in place for a break, to rest and drink water from their canteens. Shortly thereafter, they'd move out again, slowly and deliberately, on full alert with a keen sense of situational awareness.

On the other side of the knee-high dike about three feet in width, was an untended area of head-high, thick brush. It reminded Bill of the maiden cane which grew wild around his Florida hometown of Pahokee.

Bill was lead machine gunner, about eight men behind the point man. Just then, he saw guys up front go down on one knee in a precautionary stance.

"What's going on, up there?" Bill asked.

"Point man hears dinks in the bushes," came the reply from up ahead. Everyone crouched low.

"We're gonna throw grenades," came the word down the line. The men took out their grenades. Each man readied himself to throw and duck low. Then Bill heard from the brush, the unmistakable sound of a round being chambered into a rifle.

At that sound, something got into Moose Anderson. He dropped his pack, and holding his M-14, which he carried in lieu of an M-16, stepped onto the dike, bent over at the waist. "I hear that guy out there," he said.

"Moose, get off the dike!" somebody said. "We're gonna throw grenades.

"I'm gonna shoot him," said Moose, emphasizing the word "shoot."

The very next second, a four- or five-round burst came from an AK-47 maybe five or so meters away. Moose spun around to the right, then fell back off the dike. At almost the same time, the command came "Grenades! Throw grenades!"

A dozen hand grenades flew in unison from Second Platoon, each making a distinct "ping" when the spoon normally held in place by the pin, separated and fell away. About five to seven seconds later, a crescendo of loud explosions came from the brush on the other side of the dike. Dirt, leaves, and other debris flew high in the air.

Bill began firing his machine gun, spraying bursts of lead from right to left, further tearing up the weeds where the grenades had landed. As he fired maybe 100 rounds, others opened up with rifle fire. The intense firing lasted no more than a minute.

Whoever shot Moose was most likely dead. Up near the point man, somebody yelled "There's a couple running away." As two dinks ran out of the brush, two guys nearby opened up on them with M-16s, but they got away.

"Medic!" somebody yelled. The platoon medic and Lieutenant Haas came from their positions farther back in the line. The medic bent down to examine Moose. A few seconds later he said "Moose is dead. He's gone."

Lieutenant Haas got on the Prick 25. "I need an extraction," he said. "We have one Kool-Aid we need picked up." Haas then ordered the men to set up a defensive perimeter. They went through Moose's pack, taking out items they could use in the field—grenades, Claymores, and other munitions. They did not interfere with Moose's personal effects. Those would go with him.

Within 15 minutes, somebody popped smoke to guide the extraction bird to the landing zone in the rice paddy. Four guys grabbed Moose's still-uncovered body, each holding an arm or a leg, and pushed him into the chopper.

Spec. 4 Steven Richard Anderson was a tall, husky guy, which is why they called him "Moose." A bit over six feet, with short, thinning blonde hair, and a light-brown mustache, Moose was on his way home.

There were no confirmed enemy kills that day, and no weapons recovered. Moose got shot. Grenades got thrown. And not long afterward, Second Platoon was again humping the boonies, but without Moose now. That's the way it went in Vietnam. First there was quiet, then a firefight in which people would be killed. A chopper would come in to pick up their remains. Those left behind would continue as they had before, minus the dead, of course.

That night they set up a perimeter at the base of the mountains. Naturally, they talked about Moose. Everyone agreed he was a fighter, and how it was a shame to lose him. Second Platoon's fight continued, but Moose's fight was over.

Later, as Bill lay in the darkness by his machine gun, wrapped in his poncho liner, he thought about Moose. He recalled the listening post incident a few days earlier, and how Moose had gone with them, and helped bring back Giles, Legitt, and the other man.

Bill pondered how abrupt death could be. Moose was here one second, and gone the next. Bill knew he had to make every day count because any day could be his last. Back in the world, there was always a chance of dying. Maybe you'd get hit by a car, or drown, or just drop dead. None of these things, however, was likely. A healthy young man could pretty much count on being alive at day's end. But here in the boonies of Vietnam, a lot of things could happen to get you killed. Each day brought a new scenario. How that scenario played out determined whether you lived or died.

The next morning, after a C-ration breakfast, Delta Company continued into the high mountains. They reminded Bill of North Carolina's Smoky Mountains—green, steep, and heavily wooded. Each platoon took turns as the lead, penetrating ever deeper into the hills and the dense, tropical forest. The limited vision ahead and to the flanks made everyone uneasy.

Later, the point man went around a trail corner and walked unknowingly into an abandoned enemy encampment, an open area about the size of a baseball-diamond infield, where low branches on trees had been removed and underbrush had been cleared out. The thick forest had so well hidden the clearing, you couldn't tell the encampment was there until you were right up on it. Further, the dense tree canopy concealed it from the air, creating an ingenious spot for an NVA bivouac, one large enough for perhaps 200 men. There were scars on trees where NVA hammocks had hung, and several old latrines. Here and there were small fire pits soldiers had no doubt used for cooking.

Bill imagined them warming their fish and rice balls. "I guess they don't like cold food either," he thought. In spite of the evidence left behind, no one could answer the big and obvious questions—how many had been here, and where did they go?

If there were any doubts the NVA were in these mountains, the presence of this camp dispelled them all. The newly acquired knowledge of how easy it would be to walk into a large concentration of enemy troops served as a rude wake-up call.

One particular night in the mountains, Ronnie Williams and Bill shared a shallow foxhole. The earth was hard packed, making digging a challenge. The idea of a whole company of NVA stumbling up on them during the night motivated them to scrape away as much soil as they could, their only digging tools being steel pot helmets and Bill's knife. Their foxhole was nothing more than a mild indention in the earth, maybe 18 inches deep, if that.

That night, all was quiet, until about 0100, when Ronnie, a normally calm guy, suddenly flew up out of the hole, extremely agitated. Bill had no idea what was going on, but based on Ronnie's demeanor, he knew something was up, and it wasn't good.

"What's the matter?" Bill asked, as he also jumped up.

"There's a snake in the hole," said Ronnie, who hardly ever used profanity, although this would have been a good time to do so.

"A snake!" said Bill.

"Something crawled over my leg," said Ronnie

Vietnam had lots of venomous snakes, including cobras, vipers, and kraits. Some species were nicknamed "two-step Charlie," because the rumor was they'd bite you and you'd be dead before you could take two steps. As if the NVA weren't enough to worry about, the thought of being snake bitten only added to one's concerns.

Using a red-lensed military flashlight, Ronnie shone it into the hole, finding a large, thick worm, not a centipede, more like an earthworm, about a foot and a half long.

"I've never seen a worm this big," said Ronnie. "Everything over here is big. You could sell these back in Louisiana and get rich. When I get back home, I'm gonna figure out how to raise these things." Ronnie scooped up the worm and threw it into the woods. The rest of the night was quiet.

On 27 Feb, after a few days in the field with no encounters of NVA, an intense firefight broke out up ahead. Another company in the battalion, on the opposite side of the hill Delta Company was on, had engaged the NVA who were positioned on high ground one hill distant. A valley separated the opposing forces. Machine-gun fire, rifle fire, and sundry explosions from grenades and B-40 rockets emanated from the hill's far side, reverberating throughout the entire area.

Instead of charging across the valley and up the NVA's hill, the Army chose to use airpower to knock out the enemy, then use troops to mop up what was left. Delta Company, removed as they were, was scattered by platoons on parts of the hill away from the fight.

With packs off and waiting for the airstrikes, the men of Second Platoon rested under a dense forest canopy which largely obscured their view of the sky. Some used the time to eat or sip from their canteens. One guy was warming a can of Beanie Weenies, as the sounds of F-4 Phantom jets came thundering overhead.

F-4s normally came in sorties of two. First, they'd make a high bombing run, followed by a low strafing run.

On the F-4s' bombing run, Bill and the others heard the distinct clicking sounds directly overhead made by each dropped bomb as its stabilization fins popped open and snapped into place. Going the same speed as the aircraft, the bomb would glide underneath it for a distance before slamming into its target.

On the strafing runs, the sounds of each F-4's 20-millimeter Gatling gun could be heard even from a distance. Instead of the short bursts that normally came from Bill's machine gun, an F-4's Gatling gun let loose a sustained and rapid hail of bullets, a constant and solid drawl of fire, spraying the ground below with massive amounts of lead.

"Those jet jockeys are giving them hell. Go for it, boys. Anything you do, we don't have to," said one guy.

"I hope they bomb the hell out of them," said another. "The more they kill, the less we'll have to deal with them."

As the first sortie of jets peeled away, the second came in. Those in Second Platoon were facing away from their hillside, meaning they also faced away from the battle on the hill's other side. When one of the newly arrived jets came streaking toward the battle on its bombing run, Bill and probably everyone else in Second Platoon, heard a bomb's click, not overhead, but this time directly in front of them. "That doesn't sound right," someone said. They immediately knew the bomb was heading straight to where they were.

The bomb's massive and deafening explosion threw dirt, fiber, and other debris high into the air. Leaves and limbs fell from the overhead canopy. Bill's ears rang and he felt as if he'd been slugged in the stomach. The powerful percussion knocked the wind right out of him, and the contaminated air literally choked him. He struggled to breathe.

The others were in similar shape. Many were holding their ears. Momentarily disoriented, at least they were alive and relatively unhurt.

Rather than coming in right on top of them, the bomb had hit around the hill's curvature, so they were mostly shielded by the mountainside.

The blast knocked out the overhead canopy, giving them a view of the sky. What they saw was terrifying. The jet which had bombed them had circled around and was coming in low for its gun run. "My God. He's gonna strafe us!" someone yelled.

The only cover was a rocky clump of dirt, neck high and maybe 10 feet long. Several guys ran to get behind it. Lieutenant Haas yelled, "Scatter out! Scatter out! Don't clump up together."

"There ain't but one rock, Lieutenant. This is all we got," said someone. The sense of panic was overwhelming. How do you defend against an F-4?

"Pop smoke! Pop smoke!" someone yelled. At that moment, 10 to 15 smoke grenades went off, sending purple, green, red, and yellow smoke up through the air. The smoke's strong chemical smell permeated the area. The F-4 was coming in low and straight at them.

At the last second, the jet abruptly climbed into the sky. Bill could see its silver belly as it ascended. The heat from its engine saturated the platoon. Men were once again choking and gagging, as the jet peeled off to the left, made a big circle, and disappeared.

"We just about got shredded," someone said.

"Hell, I lost my Beanie Weenies," said the guy who'd been looking forward to the C-ration favorite, the anticipation of which momentarily seemed to take precedence over the brief but intense shock and terror they had just endured.

Lieutenant Haas went around to see if anyone had been wounded. Everyone in Second Platoon was intact, but cries of intense pain could be heard from around the hillside. "They got hit," said Lieutenant Haas. "An entire squad was taken out." As it turned out, there was one death, that of Private First Class Paul James Miller from Poplar Bluff, Missouri. Everyone else was wounded. Some lost limbs.

Lieutenant Haas had received word over the Prick 25 that the platoon around the hillside had sent all their squads except one down the hill to cut an LZ for resupply choppers. The one squad hit had stayed behind to guard the area.

Lieutenant Haas said the order was for Second Platoon to remain in place. The plan was the other platoon would take care of its own wounded. All morning DUSTOFFs came and went, using the same LZ that had been cut for resupply. Remaining in place as ordered, Second Platoon bivouacked that night on their side of the hill.

They spent the next few days humping the mountains, and thick jungles, without engaging the enemy. Still, distant but brief sounds of rifle fire erupted now and then, reminding everyone to remain wary.

Bill at the end of the Tet offensive

CHAPTER 21.
STAND-DOWN AT BONG SON

One morning, word came that Delta Company was going in for a stand-down. Instead of heading back to Duc Pho, they'd be going south to Bong Son, to Delta Company's new base camp. The word of a stand-down elated everyone. After a month in the field, the thought of a shower, hot chow, clean clothes, beer, and steaks made everyone jubilant.

February had been an intense and bloody month. Eight men from Delta Company were killed, and many more wounded. Delta Company lost 40 percent of its fighting capacity. Still, the Tet counteroffensive proved effective. The NVA's losses were much heavier, forcing them to withdraw from the cities back to sanctuaries to the west.

Around 0800 or 0900 on the morning of departure, choppers landed in an open area of waist-high grass at the base of the mountains to ferry the men to Highway 1. Everyone was relaxed and happy as they climbed aboard. Since he had a machine gun, Bill was seated by the chopper door, facing out, so he could provide extra firepower if necessary.

It was a bright, clear day. The mountains were lush and green, looking from the air like an inviting tropical paradise. Yet, somewhere amidst all the beauty below was the enemy. "Beauty and the beast," Bill thought as he stared below.

From the next chopper over, guys were waving and flashing "thumbs up" signs back to Bill's chopper, an outward reflection of their inner celebratory feelings. To Bill it felt as if the home team had won a championship football game. Instead of going to the dance after the game, they were headed back for a relatively cushy few days at base camp.

As bad as things had been, they could have been a lot worse. They could have been wiped out in that village, or shredded by friendly jets. In spite of that jet accident, air power had made all the difference. It had kept the NVA off them. Now was the time to feel victorious.

The 20-minute chopper ride ended when they set down in a large open area by Highway 1. Trucks were waiting to pick them up, and take them south to Bong Son. Each man climbed aboard any truck which had room. Platoons were all mixed up within the company, but it didn't matter. Bill found a spot facing the villages and rice paddies.

The ride south took them across the same bridges they had guarded a few months earlier, before Hollenbach, the milkman of bridge guard, was killed. With their trucks proceeding at only about 20 miles per hour, Bill started to recognize familiar landmarks. Bridge guard had been one of the few opportunities to interact with the locals. He remembered the children, how Hollenbach had poured them milk every morning, and how old Papa-san had often stopped by for a visit.

Little Vietnamese children now ran alongside the trucks, hoping someone would throw C-rations to them, as troops sometimes did. Many of the locals jumped up and down and waved as they recognized the guys on the convoy who had been on bridge guard near that village in October. They pitched coconuts and bananas to the trucks, fresh food as a sign of continued appreciation. The kids from the milk stop were there, shouting and waving. There was a spirit of camaraderie in the air between soldiers and the people, the result of weeks of mutual respect and courtesy. Even old Papa-san was there. Ronnie Williams, right next to Bill in the back of the truck, said "I never knew about that old man. He might have been VC for all I know, but I had to like that guy."

The base camp at Bong Son, called LZ English, was well established. It had mess halls, an infirmary, and separate clubs for officers, NCO's, and enlisted men.

Sleeping quarters were quite luxurious compared to what an infantry-man had in the field. Instead of a hole in the ground for a bed and a poncho liner for bedding, each man now had a proper cot housed inside a large tent with wooden sides and a wooden floor. Sandbags outside the tent shielded those inside from the flying shrapnel of a possible mortar attack. The canvas roof would not protect, however, from a mortar dropping directly into the tent, but close by were sandbag bunkers you could run to if necessary.

Eight-seater latrines atop split 50-gallon drums provided ample accommodations, certainly preferable to a cardboard box inside a field bunker. Urinals consisted of a section of PVC pipe stuck in the ground.

Fifty-gallon drums on stands overhead, and a series of showerheads, provided falling water for showers.

Mess halls served hot chow. The men went by platoons through the serving line to receive a plastic plate filled with food, and utensils. With no sit-down area, they simply found a spot to enjoy their hot meal.

In the field, Delta Company's platoons had been separate, but here at LZ English there were opportunities to visit with friends from other platoons.

Evenings were casual. One could buy a beer using military pay certificates, or "MPCs" as they were called. To keep American greenbacks out of black-market circulation, troops were not allowed to have U.S. currency, so they were issued MPCs instead. Possessing U.S. currency was subjected to what's called an "Article 15," or "non-judicial punishment." MPCs would buy a Carling Black Label or a Ballantine beer at the enlisted men's club. Officers at their club could buy a Miller High Life or a Coors.

LZ English had quite a history, having been a former post for the French Foreign Legion. The concrete bunkers there were built by the French, and resembled World-War-II bunkers found in Europe. After the French, it had served as a base camp for the 173rd Airborne Brigade, and the First Cavalry Division.

The first day of the stand-down, each platoon was briefed on what they had accomplished, where they had gone, whom they had fought, the number of casualties, and what they did right as well as what they did wrong. Each man got an opportunity to add input about what could have been done differently, or better.

A memorial service the following day honored Delta Company's eight men who had made the ultimate sacrifice during the Tet offensive: Spec. 4 Gregory Thomas Iding, age 20, from Cincinnati, Ohio; Spec. 4 Jose G. Cortez, age 20 from Corpus Christi, Texas; Private First Class Norman Charles Kissinger, age 22, from Milwaukee, Wisconsin; Private First Class James Garrett Miller, age 21, from Akron, Ohio; Private First Class Charles Peter Torliatt, age 20, from Petaluma, California; Spec. 4 Robert Wayne Seaton, age 22 from Kevil, Kentucky; Spec. 4 Steven Richard Anderson, age 23, from Levittown, New York; and Private First Class Paul James Miller, age 20, from Poplar Bluff, Missouri.

Each man was represented by an M-16 rifle propped up by its attached bayonet stuck in the ground. Atop the rifle's stock rested a helmet, and at each rifle's base was a pair of boots.

First, Captain Cosand reviewed those killed in action, telling their name, their age, their hometown, and how long they had been in service. Then the Rabbi read from the Old Testament, after which Father Hagen shared stories he remembered personally of each of "his boys," as he called them. Then the Protestant chaplain said a few words. The entire service lasted about 30 minutes. Donations of MPCs were made to each man so his family could purchase a memorial item.

After the memorial service came weapons cleaning duty, for which split 50-gallon containers of solvent were available. Weapons had been in the field for a while, and a thorough cleaning under the watchful eye of the Platoon Sergeant ensured they continued to work properly.

At 1300 hours, the men enjoyed a steak cook-out, complete with iced cold beer, either PBR or Falstaff. The official word was have a good time, enjoy the party, but don't get drunk.

Captain Cosand told the men "You've been in the most intense fighting in the Vietnam War. The NVA tried to take the war to the cities by violating a truce which they themselves had requested. We drove them back to their sanctuaries in Cambodia and Laos. The VC have been smashed as an effective fighting force. Throughout the country, the NVA have been defeated. Be proud of yourselves, just as I am proud of you."

Then the good Captain went around and spoke with each soldier separately. He knew everyone's name, and treated each man as an individual. Going up to John Gentry, Cosand put his hand on Gentry's shoulder, shook Gentry's hand and said. "Gentry, you're a great soldier. I can always count on you to do what needs to be done. This man's Army is better off because of men like you."

"Thank you, Captain," said Gentry with a blank look on his face. As Cosand went to the next guy, Gentry's blank look remained, but now a couple of tears fell from his eyes. "That's the first time any officer has ever talked to me and said anything nice," Gentry said.

Later that day, Lieutenant Haas gave an overview of who was wounded, and announced that replacements would be coming in. As for future assignments, one platoon would be guarding bridges in the Bong Son area. The other two were to provide security for artillery units on Firebases Geronimo and Laramie. He told the men they would be on LZ English for two more days. During that time, they should visit the dentist, the chaplain, the infirmary for jungle rot, or whoever else they needed to see for whatever reason.

The men exchanged dirty clothes for clean ones, which had been delivered to the company area. At night they watched TV shows outdoors—Bonanza and Gunsmoke—which were projected onto a white sheet hung against one of the buildings. They were even allowed to drink beer while doing so. The whole thing reminded Bill of going to the drive-in theater back home, but here there was no sweet-smelling girl to share the experience with.

It was fun to be clean on a daily basis, something the men of Delta Company hadn't known for a long time.

Care packages came from family and friends, including the always-welcomed packages from FSU's AOPi girls. The men shared what they had with one another.

During this down time, they wrote letters, and read paperback books, especially James Bond books.

The chaplains, including Father Hagen, went from hooch to hooch to see if anyone wanted to talk or pray. Father Hagen didn't ask anyone's religion. He'd put his hand on their shoulder, bow his head, and pray for them.

The next afternoon, Lieutenant Haas called a meeting of Second Platoon to explain the nature of Delta Company's new assignment on LZ Geronimo, located about 17 klicks north of LZ English. After that, the Company would be on LZ Laramie, about 10 klicks west-northwest of English. With the men gathered around informally, he explained that these were established artillery outposts which provided supporting fire for the 1st Cavalry Division and the 173rd Airborne Brigade. Delta Company would be patrolling around these firebases looking for enemy activity.

Now short about 40 men, Delta would continue this assignment at least until replacements came in.

Leaving the field after Tet for the stand-down at Bong Son

Cliff Torrey displays a captured B-40 rocket launcher at the Bong Son
stand-down. More NVA captured weapons in the background.

CHAPTER 22.
FIREBASES GERONIMO
AND LARAMIE

At mid-morning the following day, around 10 Hueys, accompanied by Huey gunships came to ferry understrength Delta Company to Firebase Geronimo, only about 5 klicks due west of the coast, and about 7 klicks southwest of Sa Huynh where Bill had spent Christmas and New Year. As Bill's chopper approached Geronimo for a landing, one of the Warrant Officer pilots said "Okay, get off guys. This is going to be your home for a while."

Bill was grateful this landing was not a combat assault like they had experienced on Hardcore. As the choppers gently set down, the men quickly exited their aircrafts. Taking care not to get beheaded by rotors, they ran away from the chopper pad, after which they followed a trail to an area of bunkers maybe 50 feet down the hill at the firebase.

For Delta Company, time on LZ Geronimo turned out to be almost like an R&R. Permanent bunkers built by Army combat engineers served as sleeping quarters. An Army field kitchen served hot chow three times a day. The extent of Delta's duties was to patrol the hill for a couple of hours each day, not an intimidating task. This was a secure hill, and was never mortared or attacked during Delta's stay.

After a few days, Delta Company went by Chinook from LZ Geronimo to LZ Laramie, high in the mountains, overlooking the same river valley where they had fought the 22nd NVA Regiment back in November. Located both on and near the apex of a barren ridgeline strewn with huge black boulders, LZ Laramie was dotted with dozens of sandbagged bunkers, mostly long, low, and flat-topped, and arranged haphazardly along the ridge's crest.

Besides the numerous bunkers, Bill saw the Tactical Operations Center, or the TOC (tock) as they called it, a rectangular sandbagged bunker with big antennas protruding from its steel-supported roof which was covered with at least two layers of sandbags. The sturdy construction was the work of Army engineers who designed it to withstand even a direct mortar hit, although a B-40 rocket might have penetrated it. Inside the TOC, officers, probably Captains and maybe a Major in this case, strategized field operations, and communicated with others at distant locations. Using their radios, they could reach Qui Nhon some 85 klicks to the south-southeast, and An Khe, about 70 klicks to the south-southwest. The TOC was an important nerve center for operations in the area. Dink forward observers might recognize it by its antennas, making it a prime target, so it had to be as secure as possible.

The word was that Delta Company would be on 24-hour alert here, with no down time at all. They'd patrol off the hillside, making sure the enemy didn't mess with the artillery, a battery of 155 mm Howitzers the reports of which would cause the whole hill to shake. The loud noises and shakes the big guns made often caused newly arrived guys sitting in their bunkers to think the hill had been hit by incoming rounds.

Part of Delta's duty would be to man the posts set up about 100 meters beyond the perimeter. These posts were established bunkers which functioned as observation posts during the day and listening posts at night. Each squad would take turns manning these bunkers.

All in all, LZ Laramie turned out to be good duty. The mail came, bringing care packages from home. There were bunkers to sleep in. There was hot chow, and established latrines. There were no firefights. In fact, Delta Company never interacted with the enemy there at all. Both Geronimo and Laramie proved to be a good places to bring in replacements and acclimate them to a combat zone. Among the new replacements were Arnold Lovelace, Eddie Bolton, Sam Agius, Billy Boetje, and Frank Belcher.

After a couple of days on Laramie, Lieutenant Haas called Bill to the CP and told him "You're going on a trip, leaving us for a while."

Bill's first thought was that maybe something was wrong at home, but that wasn't it.

Haas explained to him that he'd been selected to go to Brigade NCO School at LZ English. Each platoon got to pick one man to attend. "We need new Sergeants," said Haas. "You've done well. I've seen you in action, and you're our pick. You'll be in school for two weeks. You're in the channel to be a Sergeant. You'll learn more about mapping and fire support. You'll be flying to Bong Son tomorrow."

Firebase Laramie

The reports of the 155 Howitzer on Firebase Laramie shook the whole hill. Notice the big gun's right tire off the ground as it recoils from the fire.

CHAPTER 23.
BRIGADE AND DIVISION
NCO SCHOOLS

The next day Bill and Cliff Torrey caught the resupply chopper to LZ English. Cliff was a draftee, a hardcore surfer from San Diego who could talk surfer talk with the best of them. He thought the Vietnam War was a real bummer. Bill had met him at Tiger Land. In spite of his negative feelings for the war, Torrey was an outstanding soldier. He had been decorated with an Army commendation medal for valor for pursuing some Viet Cong while on bridge guard in October, capturing enemy weapons in the process.

During the two weeks at NCO school, Bill learned how to call in artillery and air strikes. Months spent in the field had taught him that the ability to call for fire support was a vital skill. In addition, Bill learned patrolling, and map-and-compass skills. The knowledge he gained would help his squad or platoon survive in the field.

The only downside Bill could see to NCO school was having to spit-shine his boots. He thought the shiny-boots requirement in Vietnam was a joke. Still, polishing boots beat climbing mountains and fighting with NVA and VC.

After two weeks of rigid inspections and spit shines, on 23 March 1968, Bill graduated 7th in his class of 20 men. According to his scores, he would have been 4th, but he lost a few points because he unintentionally pissed off some Sergeant. Cliff Torrey, the California surfer, distinguished himself by coming in first place.

After graduation, Bill was selected to go to Division NCO School at Camp Enari, which meant two more weeks of instruction. Camp Enari, a self-contained military city located about 10 klicks south of Pleiku, served as headquarters for the entire 4th Infantry Divison.

Within its boundaries was the 71st Evacuation Hospital, a complete motor pool, ammo dumps, an engineer company, and a maintenance company. Command centers contained a General and his staff. The area was mostly flat, except for nearby Dragon Mountain, where lots of communications equipment and personnel were located. Bunkers fortified the perimeter, as did big spot lights, M60A1 tanks, concertina wire, and mine fields. Military Police and other soldiers pulled bunker guard as part of their daily duties. Camp Enari was as secure as possible, under the circumstances. Still, it was vulnerable to mortar and rocket attacks. Strong and well-built bunkers located outside many of the buildings, especially those where people slept, provided a potential refuge in case of incoming rounds.

During the dry season, the red clay soil of Camp Enari turned to nasty dust, to be blown about by the wind. When the monsoon rains came, the red dust turned to sticky mud.

Division NCO school had its own small campus, complete with a mess hall, and a barracks which housed the trainees. Instructors treated their trainees with respect without the usual military harassment Bill had experienced in other training situations. They wanted to pass on useful information that could be truly helpful in the field.

The men learned things such as where the VC would likely place booby traps, the different types of booby traps, and ways the VC would try to psyche out our soldiers to place their traps. Around Pleiku, for example, there was little shade, unlike the jungle areas in which Bill had recently been. You might decide, for example, to take a break under a prominent shade tree. The VC had learned to anticipate your actions, making the area under that tree a likely spot for a trap. "Where you go to sit on your ass, is where Charlie's going to blow your ass away," explained one instructor.

The men also got first-hand scenario-based training on the finer points of setting up a company perimeter. "You're the Platoon Leader," or "You're the Platoon Sergeant," the instructor would say. "Where are you going put your CP?"

The training was more hands-on, more practical application, than what Bill had received at Brigade NCO School, which had been mostly classroom instruction. Here, they were in the field, walking several klicks per day, armed with M-16s and plenty of ammo. The area was flat and open, and they never felt intimidated.

They also learned to call in medevacs, and were introduced to the use of scout dogs. The level of instruction at Division NCO School took Bill to a higher level of thinking.

They had free time after schooling sessions to go to the ville near Pleiku, by catching a truck into town. Everywhere they went, however, they carried an M-16, a bandolier of ammo, and their steel-pot helmet, even around Camp Enari. Being armed was part of who you were.

Nighttime entertainment included outdoor movies, and meals at the EM club or the USO. The USO featured young, college-aged women, Red Cross volunteers who had left their lives back in the world to come boost the morale of soldiers serving in the war. "Donut dollies" they were called, because they often brought donuts as gifts to the troops. They wore light blue uniforms, and usually sported short, perky hair. They would talk to you like a girl back home would. Their presence in the midst of war made life better.

Bill met two Canadians at Division NCO school. They were Canadian citizens who had enlisted in the U.S. Army to fight in Vietnam. When they finished their tour, they planned to go back to Canada.

After weeks of instruction, at both the Brigade and the Division levels, not to mention practical lessons gained from months in combat, Bill graduated from the 4th Division's NCO School on 5 April, prepared to be a combat-infantry Sergeant.

CHAPTER 24. DARING ROAD TRIP

After graduaton, Bill and several men from other battalions learned that their Third Brigade Task Force would be moving from its base camp at LZ English, near Bong Son, to LZ Mary Lou near Kontum. Since Kontum was only about 45 klicks north of Pleiku, they had the option of remaining at secure Camp Enari and rejoining their group which would come through the area in a few days on their way from Bong Son to Kontum.

The NCO-School grads had heard, however, that back at Bong Son, the guys were having a stand-down after coming in from the field. That meant kicking back, eating steaks, drinking beer, and spending time with buddies from their own units. Hanging around Camp Enari meant pulling guard duty, or maybe even shit-burning details.

As it turned out, they discussed the situation with a couple of truck drivers who agreed to take them to Bong Son. The drivers often went back and forth from Pleiku to Bong Son in large convoys, so they were familiar with the route.

Having checked out of Camp Enari, the NCO grads and their drivers set out in a two-truck convoy along Highway 19 early in the morning of 7 April on a daring 200-kilometer road trip which would take them east through the infamous Mang Yang Pass where the Viet Minh had ambushed French forces in June of 1954, slaughtering them by the hundreds. That monumental defeat for the French was the last major battle of the First Indo-China War. The following month, an armistice ended the conflict, and divided Vietnam at the 17th parallel, creating North and South Vietnam.

Passing first through Pleiku, Bill noticed the town's square, and the market area with its little businesses scattered up and down the road. Going east out of Pleiku, the road opened up into a relatively flat agricultural area.

Soon the two lone trucks, carrying about a dozen young Americans armed only with M-16s, headed straight into the dreaded Mang Yang pass. Tensions mounted as they approached it. The road took them through a deep valley with steep, jungled mountains on either side. Everything about the Mang Yang Pass screamed "ambush." But talking about it among themselves, the guys rationalized the NVA or the VC wouldn't waste a good ambush on only two trucks. They'd hold out for better prey. Plus, they did see American soldiers with rifles on bulldozers along the road side. That military presence gave them at least some peace of mind. They then saw numerous people moving around on the top of one of the hills. Were they Americans or NVA? At that moment the big question arose, "What the hell are we doing here?" They hoped they were Americans providing security for the pass, but were not sure.

With an ample amount of dumb luck, the daring two-truck convoy drove uneventfully the three or four kilometers through the Mang Yang Pass, and continued east to the town of An Khe. In the downtown area, they saw active markets, with industrious, enterprising vendors selling vegetables, pigs, chickens, plus a variety of pots, pans and other merchandise. The local citizens whizzed by on motor scooters and bicycles. Ponies plodded along pulling wagons loaded with people and their belongings. Lovely, well-groomed young Vietnamese girls with long, dark hair and tight silk dresses split up the side walked in groups of two or three. The guys wanted to stay and look around An Khe but their time was limited because come what may, they had to be in Bong Son by dark.

Leaving An Khe, they continued toward the infamous An Khe Pass, more mountainous terrain where Americans were often ambushed. They saw no large convoys of U.S. vehicles, but occasionally a Vietnamese minivan would go by, sometimes with people sitting atop. Highway 19 was a major transportation corridor linking the Central Highlands with the coast. A few civilian trucks passed by loaded with crates, boxes, and other cargo. Most were, no doubt, headed to Pleiku.

The mood in the convoy was calm as they approached the An Khe Pass. After all, they had made it through the Mang Yang. Surely, the An Khe would be no problem. They drove along briskly through the pass, drinking beer, enjoying the countryside, not intimidated at all, feeling more like tourists than combat soldiers. Still, the higher ground along the roadside suggested the possibility of an ambush.

Within a few minutes, they were safely through the pass, and on their way to Qui Nhon. On the outskirts of the city, they came upon a military checkpoint, manned by South Koreans forces, or ROKs as they were called, which stood for "Republic of Korea." The ROKs were ferocious fighters, efficient and formidable. They were well dressed and looked militarily sharp. By all appearances, they were sturdy and capable soldiers. The NVA and VC were particularly afraid of the ROKs. There were rumors of ROKs beheading enemy dead, then displaying those heads on stakes as a warning about the extent of brutality that awaited anyone who dared tangle with them. Some said the ROKs were stationed at Qui Nhon because it was secure. Others, however, thought Qui Nhon was secure because the last thing the NVA wanted was to confront the ROKs.

At the checkpoint, half a dozen ROK soldiers carefully inspected each of the two trucks.

"I wonder if those guys know what a Playboy magazine is," one of the Americans said.

At that suggestion, someone pulled out a recent copy of Playboy and showed it to the ROKs, who took great delight in the naked forms of young women depicted in all their physical beauty. The Koreans wanted to keep the magazine, so the young Americans saw a chance for a trade—a case of Korean Crown beer for a Playboy. Once everyone understood the terms of the trade, it was a done deal.

The convoy set out resupplied on their way to Bong Son, making one more stop outside Qui Nhon, this time at a military refueling station called a POL, which stood for "petroleum, oils, and lubricants." They topped their tanks, signed the log book, giving the info as to their unit and destination. They bought sandwiches and cold drinks from one of the vendors surrounding the POL site.

This bit of normalcy—stopping at what was essentially a roadside truck stop and getting food—was quite a treat for these young men who had spent so much time in harsh conditions in the boonies.

Still near Qui Nhon, Bill spotted a small Catholic church, made of brick and mortar, with a large cross in front. A cluster of people gathered around it, including nuns in their black habits. The presence of this church and its people made Bill think they were in a fairly protected and secure area.

Next, they followed Highway 1 north to Bong Son, and before too long crossed the river bridge south of the town. Bong Son looked every bit a thriving tropical town, with lots of commercial activity and boulevards lined on each side with tall and impressive coconut palms. Crossing the wide and well-constructed steel bridge, Bill looked at the river below and saw people wading in the water, doing laundry, and fishing.

Knowing the way, the drivers negotiated town traffic, finding LZ English with no problem. Upon arriving at the gate near dark, the guard greeted them with the news that the stand-down party was over, and those in the 1st of the 14th had flown out on C-130s earlier in the day to Kontum. Rear-echelon troops had remained to pack up the gear in preparation for leaving. Inside the gate, Bill saw trucks and trailers already loaded with equipment, ready for the road trip to Pleiku, and then on to Kontum.

Tension mounts as Spec. 4 Ruby and Spec. 4 Lovely ride through the Mang Yang pass

CHAPTER 25. AMBUSH AT AN KHE

Two days later, a 50-truck convoy left LZ English, bound this day for An Khe, where they bivouacked for the night, and enjoyed a refreshing afternoon swim in the clear, cool waters of the An Khe River.

On leaving An Khe the next morning, they allowed a small convoy to go ahead of them. About 5 or 10 klicks west of An Khe, that convoy was ambushed by NVA.

The entire 50-truck convoy stopped and waited while elements of the 173rd Airborne Brigade made a chopper combat assault on the enemy. In only a matter of minutes, tanks, APCs, gunships, and jets were in the area.

Those in the 50-truck convoy could only watch from where they were. Sitting on the cabs of their trucks, they observed the fighting through binoculars, seeing the 173rd sweep the area. Enterprising civilians from nearby settlements soon came out on bikes to sell Cokes and beer to the troops watching the fighting. Some sold souvenirs. One guy bought a crossbow with the idea of sending it home. Prostitutes, called "boom-boom girls," rode in pairs on motor scooters, offering their services for a mere $5 MPC. While most of the troops declined their offers, a few were seen following one of the boom-boom girls into the bushes.

To Bill, the whole thing seemed surreal. Here they were, drinking beer and Cokes, buying souvenirs from ambitious Vietnamese entrepreneurs, and some were even getting laid, all while watching a war through binoculars. This wasn't like anything he had ever imagined about war.

He thought about how the Vietnamese people had survived decades of war and in the process had adapted to war to enhance their income.

In World War II, the Japanese ran the French out, and occupied Vietnam. When the Japanese surrendered in 1945, and the Rising Sun Empire ended, they left Vietnam, and the French returned. The French fought several Vietnamese independence movements involving multiple armies, including Ho Chi Minh's large army, and several small armies, all of which had in common that they didn't want to be returned to French rule. The French, after their 1954 defeats at Dien Bien Phu and the Mang Yang Pass, withdrew from French Indo-China, which included not only Vietnam but also Laos and Cambodia. Cultural, religious, and political differences divided the north of Vietnam from the south part of the country. Coinciding with the French exodus, a Geneva Conference in 1954 formally but temporarily divided Vietnam at the 17th parallel. The idea was they'd have an election in 1956 to determine who would rule the country. The populated, communist North was confident in an electoral victory.

The U.S., however, following the Truman Doctrine, under which communism would be contained, did not want to see another country fall to the red menace. When the South Vietnamese people asked the U.S. for military, financial, and political assistance, President Eisenhower was sympathetic to their cause, and sent military advisors to help. Later, President John F. Kennedy, who also supported maintaining a non-communist government in South Vietnam, created a Special Forces group called the Green Berets. He sent them to the Republic of Vietnam to live among the people, to help organize, train, and maintain an effective fighting force against communist insurgents financed and equipped by the North, China, and Russia.

A few years later, Bill and half million other American troops were here to carry out Eisenhower's and Kennedy's plan for a non-communist South Vietnam. That's how Bill was now on this road, watching this battle, and watching these local Vietnamese people in their daily activities of making a living from the turmoil of war.

Four hours later, the 50-truck convoy continued west toward Pleiku. Passing the ambush site, Bill saw one destroyed U.S. truck, a civilian bus riddled with bullet holes, and a lot of dead and wounded civilians. Several medevac choppers came in to retrieve the wounded. Bill didn't see any wounded or dead Americans, but someone later said that two U.S. soldiers had been wounded.

As for the attacking NVA, they got hammered. Dozens of dead NVA were stacked on APCs, along with piles of AK-47s. Bill told his driver to slow down so he could snap a photo with his Instamatic camera. As he was taking the photo, he asked the soldiers standing next to the vehicle, which displayed a State of Indiana flag on its whip antenna, what they planned to do with the bodies.

One of them said, "Buddy, we're taking these gooks and are gonna dump 'em in the An Khe town square so the Viet Cong sympathizers can see what happens when the NVA or VC ambush a convoy. They get their asses killed."

Other than getting soaked by an early monsoon rain, the convoy reached Pleiku with no trouble at all. Two days later, Bill flew by Chinook to Kontum, where he enjoyed an all-day bull session with Ronnie Williams who had come in from the field to DEROS (Date of Estimated Return from Overseas) back to the states. Then, Bill and a friend nicknamed "Gomer" explored downtown Kontum, which had been hit hard during the Tet offensive. Entire blocks of buildings were blown apart or riddled with bullet holes. In spite of the devastation, the whole town was busy rebuilding.

Ambush ahead, a few klicks west of An Khe

CHAPTER 26. WEST OF POLEI KLENG

The next day, Bill choppered out along with three new replacements to a forward firebase about eight klicks from the Cambodian border, where Charlie Company was stationed. The four had been unable to catch a resupply bird out to join up in the boonies with their own Delta Company. So, they pulled perimeter guard duty at night as part of Charlie Company. During this time, they made no contact with the dinks. Hill 1230 was right across from their firebase. As Bill studied the high hill, he was glad he'd probably never be called to charge up it.

Being farther north, early monsoon rains had started to set in where they were. Bill thought how he enjoyed being dry in January, February, and March. Although a lot of bad stuff happened during that time, "At least," he thought, "we were dry." Being wet meant contending with biting insects, jungle rot, and leeches. He knew if they had stayed at Bong Son, he'd be dry for a few more weeks.

Thoughts of R&R increasingly occupied his mind. He'd been in country since last August, been through all kinds of shit, and a relaxing week in some place like Australia sounded more than inviting. Many of his old buddies had gone home—Ronnie Williams, Keith Raitz, Hank, Gomer, and Barham. He was already missing them. Plus, other good men were leaving this month. When Bill left to return to the field, he knew with all those going stateside, and with about 20 on sick call, Delta Company was critically low on men.

By the morning of 14 April, Easter Sunday, Bill had managed to catch a resupply bird back to Delta Company, located now somewhere in the boonies about 25 klicks west-northwest of Kontum, and also west of a place called Polei Kleng, a Special Forces camp where Green Beret troops trained indigenous soldiers in the art of warfare.

Polei Kleng was likely a prime NVA target. It had recently been catching rocket and mortar fire, so protecting it was high priority. As part of that protection, understrength Delta Company, now with only about 60 men instead of the usual 130 or so, humped the jungle ridgelines looking for NVA.

That afternoon, the men were told to set up a perimeter because a chopper was coming in. In a few minutes, the chopper set down in a grassy area. To the men's pleasant surprise, ruddy-cheeked Irish Father Hagen and his slight-of-build assistant exited the aircraft. The beloved Catholic chaplain had told them at the Bong Son stand-down, he'd be with them on Easter no matter where they were. Sure enough, here he was, as he had promised.

So as not to be an especially inviting target, the chopper took off leaving Father Hagen and his assistant inside the perimeter.

He told the men "I'm here to pray with you, and give you communion. Also, I have something for you no matter what your religion." It was egg nog spiked with rum.

As the men sat or kneeled in small groups around the perimeter, Father Hagen went from group to group praying with them, and offering them communion. As they'd pray, some would kneel, some would stand.

Sometimes, he would touch a man on the shoulder. "We're here," he said "to celebrate the life and resurrection of Jesus Christ."

He went on to pray for each man's safety and guidance in doing what he was here to do. He asked the Lord to be with them, their parents, and their families. He then offered the egg nog in little disposable cups he had brought for that purpose.

In less than half an hour from the chopper's departure, someone popped smoke, and the big green bird landed once more. Father Hagen along with his assistant climbed aboard.

Father Hagen, standing in the doorway, held up his hand and said "God bless these boys."

As the engines revved, and the chopper lifted off, Bill thought that it took a lot of gonads for a chaplain, a U.S. Army Major, to come out to where they were. Anything could have happened. They could have had a hot landing, or gotten shot down. Father Hagen was a priority passenger. He was the entire reason the chopper made its flight. The average Major didn't ride out to the field for half an hour, and then return. As far as Bill could recall, Father Hagen was the only Major he had seen in the boonies. His willingness to leave a relatively secure base camp and come to the boonies earned Father Hagen a tremendous amount of respect.

It seemed everyone knew Father Hagen.

CHAPTER 27. LZ MILE HIGH

The next day, 15 April, proved to be one of the many days in Vietnam Bill would never forget. As the men patrolled the jungle, in line by platoons, each man appropriately spaced one from another, the signal came to take a knee. Anytime a company stops advancing in the field, something is going on. In this case, word passed from one soldier to the next that they were going to be choppered out to replace a couple of companies badly hit earlier that day in a horrendous firefight on a firebase called LZ Mile High. The word was they'd likely be coming in on a hot LZ.

Twenty minutes later, choppers came in one at a time, and picked them up from a nearby grassy area. The flight to the LZ lasted perhaps 15 minutes. During this time, Bill reflected on the last time they'd been called to help another company in trouble. That was during Tet, and a two-day battle ensued. Below him, he saw mountains covered with thick, solid jungles.

Soon, a scarred mountaintop appeared on a distant ridgeline. This was LZ Mile High. With only one place for a helicopter to land, the choppers had to wait, coming in one at a time. Medevac choppers going out provided evidence things hadn't gone well in that day's battle. Looking down, Bill could see lots of wounded men on the ground, some being maintained with IV's.

Before landing, those in the chopper were told to run to nearby bunkers. Bill ran to a bunker about 100 feet away. There were no incoming rounds, as they had anticipated, so a small group of guys stood right outside the bunker.

Bill recognized one of them as Terry Lance, a fellow graduate from Division NCO school at Camp Enari, only 10 days prior. Leaning against the bunker, Lance had a blank look. He appeared haggard and tired.

"What happened here?" Bill asked.

Lance explained how they were there to provide security for the firebase. For several days, they'd been going on sweeps around the hill, first following the ridgeline, then sweeping down one side of the hill on one day, and the other side of the hill the next.

"Boe," he said "after going along the flank of the hill, we came back up to the ridgeline leading to the firebase, and hit a wall of shit. A couple of hundred yards out, they started shooting at us. We hit the ground. They hit us from both flanks—machine guns, hand grenades, mortars, and B-40s. The sons of bitches were shooting at us from the trees. They were like monkeys in the trees. We'd get in a prone position to return fire, and they'd shoot at us from the trees. We got all our wounded back, but we had to leave some dead guys out there. We couldn't bring them back. Had too many wounded. If you go out there, Boe, look in the trees."

Bill thought about how they had not encountered snipers in trees before, but they had never been among massive trees such as these found here closer to the Cambodian border. These weren't like oak trees or pine trees you could look into. These were huge, thick trees which could provide good concealment for anyone hiding in them.

Lance, and the rest of Charlie Company, 1/35th were evacuated out by choppers a few minutes later.

Shortly thereafter, Sergeant First Class Archambo went from bunker to bunker informing the men they'd be staying put tonight, taking Charlie Company's place. He told them they'd now be providing security for the firebase. They should be awake, be sharp, and not take anything for granted. He went on to explain to the men that their job tonight was to maintain perimeter security.

"There are NVA all around us," Archambo said. "Their job is to destroy this hill. Our job is to keep them from doing it. This is a hot hill. Expect anything at any time."

He made sure everyone had plenty of ammo, Claymores to put out, and would be awake. He told them that now was a good time to fill their canteens from the water wagon, and be sure they had C-rations.

Sergeant First Class Archambo was an E-7 career soldier, a lifer, not some "shake and bake" Sergeant who graduated from NCO school back in the states. He hadn't been in combat until his Vietnam tour, so he was experiencing the fighting just like most of the rest of his platoon. He was an excellent Platoon Sergeant, a professional with plenty of formal training. He knew what he was doing. He had joined Delta Company sometime during the Tet offensive. Most guys liked him. Whenever some troop would give him lip, calling him "Sarge" in the process, he'd remind them he was to be called "Sergeant Archambo," and they were to do what he said. He was formal as far as giving orders, but he knew each of his men, and tried his best to make sure they were doing what they were best qualified to do. At about 180 pounds, Sergeant Archambo was older and larger than most men in the company. He stood maybe six feet tall, a solid man, with inch-long brown hair, and sturdy brown-framed eyeglasses. His language, for a Sergeant, was clean, not unduly littered with profanity.

LZ Mile High was a nasty, desolate, grim hill. The bunkers were low and smelled of mildew, with no ventilation. They were only about 100 feet from the perimeter's wire, right along the edge of where the mountain dropped off directly into the thick jungle below. Ground fog rolled in during the early evening, obscuring the view. The jungle and most likely the NVA surrounded the firebase. The same people who had fought Charlie and Delta Companies, 1/35th that day were ready to fight Delta Company, 1/14th that night. No one felt secure. They knew they were in the guts of NVA territory.

The next morning, Sergeant Archambo told his men they would most likely be spending the day humping the ridge off the firebase. The plan was to go down the ridge about 800 meters, past where the ambush was, and establish a permanent listening post.

Owing to the large numbers of NVA in the area, the Battalion Commander wanted a presence off the hill. The orders were to leave a platoon to man the LP. That platoon—fewer than 30 men now due to Delta Company's reduced numbers—would be stationed in the jungle out beyond the area where two companies had been outnumbered and caught hell the day before. The plan was for Bill's platoon, Second Platoon, to be left alone to face possibly hundreds, or maybe thousands of North Vietnamese troops. Making matters worse, artillery and gunship support might not even be available.

For the first time in the war, Bill felt as if he were being asked to be expendable.

Leaving the perimeter, Bill was Squad Leader near the front with his rifle squad. They had gone only about 150 meters when they came upon the ambush site and saw bodies of young Americans littered about the trail like beer cans at a dump. Bill thought "Two entire companies got hit only 150 meters out of the perimeter, and they've ordered 55 of us to go out 800 meters, and leave our Second Platoon there?"

Bill saw three bodies in the trail, heads facing back toward LZ Mile High. Fifty feet from those three, another three bodies lay clustered around a tree. One was leaning against the tree, arms hanging by his side, head tilted back. The young man had blond hair, and crisp blue eyes, a nice-looking kid. Bill imagined he probably played high-school football, and dated a cheerleader. He thought, "That's a good-looking boy, and his mother doesn't even know he's dead yet." Bill then saw what he thought was a fatigue jacket hanging in the bushes. Upon closer inspection, he saw two arms hanging out of the jacket, with no head, and nothing below the waist.

Sergeant Archambo's face was ashen. "Boe," he asked, "did you ever think we'd see shit like this?"

"Sergeant Archie," said Bill, "I never did, and I never want to see anything like this again."

"Me either, Boe. Me either," he said.

"Where's the rest of this guy?" Bill asked Sergeant Archambo

"Boe, I don't know. I just don't know," he said.

Moving another 50 feet down the thickly jungled trail, they heard movement on the flanks. The sound reminded Bill of raccoons scampering through mangroves. They heard voices softly talking back and forth to one another in Vietnamese. The jungle was so thick, the dinks might have been no more than 10 meters away, on both sides of the trail. Archambo raised his open hand to indicate to stop. With the Prick 25 hand piece up to his ear, listening to the transmissions, he told Bill "We're trying to get artillery support for our flanks." A minute or two later, Archambo said "There's no artillery support available. We're going back to Mile High. We're going back in. They're telling us to go back, and go back briskly."

Nearing the battle area once more, Bill asked Sergeant Archambo "Are we going to be bringing the bodies back with us?"

Archambo got on the radio, and said "We're approaching the battle site. Do you want us to recover the bodies and take them back with us?" He paused a moment while listening to the radio, then said "They don't want us to get the bodies. They want us to get back to the hill."

Bill told Sergeant Archambo, "These guys shouldn't be left out here like this."

Archambo said, "I know, Boe, but we've been told to get back to the hill."

Nobody liked the idea of leaving the bodies there, but orders were orders, and they did go briskly back to the perimeter.

Once inside, Sergeant Archambo told everyone to find a cool place and take a break. "Eat some C-rations, and drink some water," he said. "We don't know what we're doing next."

At about 1500 hours, Sergeant Archambo said "It looks like they're going to send us back out there to set up that LP."

Crazy Joe, an assistant machine gunner, said he wasn't going back out. "This is crazy as shit," he said. And it did seem crazy, sending men out into a jungle full of NVA, late in the afternoon, then leaving an understrength platoon out there on their own with no fire support, no entrenching tools, and expecting them to set up a decent perimeter before dark. "I came over here to fight a war," Crazy Joe said, "not commit suicide. Boe, you ever seen a Major or Lieutenant Colonel out here?"

"Seen lots of Captains," said Bill.

"I ain't going," said Crazy Joe.

Several others joined Crazy Joe in the refusal, saying they weren't going either, even though refusal to go could lead to a court martial. But sending a small contingent of men into an area where you couldn't even bring back the dead, made no sense to the soldiers on the ground, especially since those sending them weren't even there to see the situation.

Those who refused to go were segregated from the company, and Bill never saw them again. He later heard that one of the other Company Commanders in the Battalion took Crazy Joe in as a machine gunner, and he served well in that unit for the rest of his tour. Bill had even heard that he was put in for a valor award but didn't get it due to the incident on Mile High.

The rest saddled up, and went back out. Once they reached the bodies again, they heard NVA talking again, and making rustling sounds as they pushed through the brush, shadowing the company like a bunch of panthers. Bill thought "They're probably talking among themselves, wondering where these dumbasses are going. They're probably planning to overrun us tonight."

The Company Commander got on the Prick 25, and said he didn't think this was a practical mission, and requested to be brought back. A few minutes later, the word came they were being called back to the hill, since neither artillery nor gunship support was available. Passing the bodies once more, they radioed to see about bringing them back. "No," was the order. "Get back to the hill."

The next day, a body-recovery team consisting of one rifle platoon left the hill carrying fold-up canvas stretchers and body bags. The team had been out about only half an hour when Bill saw them returning, with seven bodies on stretchers and already in bags, one man carrying each corner of a stretcher. The scene reminded Bill of pall bearers at a funeral. Everyone got quiet at the sight of the fallen being brought back. A few minutes later, somebody popped smoke for an incoming chopper, which landed, picked up the bodies, and left. The idea that the bodies had been left in the jungle for two days did not sit well with anyone.

Delta Company remained on the hill the rest of the day. Unlike some other firebases, Mile High was a somber hill. Many times, on a firebase, the sounds of AFVN radio drifted across the hill, but not on Mile High. The troops here weren't especially fearful, but they were cautious, anticipating maximum violence, knowing a major battle could erupt at any moment. Mile High was a nasty place.

LZ Mile High was a nasty place.

Body recovery team going out of LZ Mile High

CHAPTER 28.
BACK IN THE BOONIES
WEST OF POLEI KLENG

The next day, Delta Company was choppered out and set down back in the jungles west of Polei Kleng. Their mission was once again to hump the ridgelines so the NVA couldn't use these high-ground areas to launch mortars and rockets on the Special Forces camp.

They skirmished several times with the NVA, in brief firefights lasting less than a minute, but Delta Company encountered no sustained action, since the NVA would break contact. Apparently, the dinks' purpose was to go somewhere else, and not engage in jungle firefights in this part of the country.

Although there wasn't much engagement, there was indeed good evidence for significant dink activity in the area. Along the trails, the men found NVA equipment—medical pouches, canteens, bandages, and other tell-tale items which served as constant reminders that the dinks weren't far away at all.

One day, following a ridgeline trail, they came upon numerous trees on both flanks with shriveled and decayed leaves. Most trees were green and fresh, but these with their rotting leaves looked anything but healthy. Having been in the jungle for months, this was the first time they'd seen such dying vegetation.

The guy in front of Bill asked "How come there's no leaves?"

"I've heard they're spraying defoliants on the ridgelines," said Bill. "They're spraying some stuff down in the Delta to remove cover so the enemy can't use it to hide."

In this case, the Army was spraying the ridgelines around Polei Kleng to be able to spot the enemy from the air. The idea was instead of having infantry troops hike back and forth to find the dinks, helicopter gunships could locate them by scouting the ridgelines.

At night, Delta would set up a company perimeter on a ridgeline, putting out lots of Claymores and trip flares. The hard ground prevented digging foxholes, so the men took up positions behind trees.

Besides the normal challenges of living with the threat of abrupt combat, Delta Company now faced an additional challenge—a severe water shortage. On a firebase, water was usually available from water wagons brought in by Chinooks. In the low-land boonies, the troops often found water in rice paddies, streams, or lakes. In these instances, they'd cover the mouth of their canteen with a piece of cloth to deflect any chunky bits while filling it. They'd then add an iodine tablet to the full canteen of water, and maybe top it off with powdered Kool-Aid to kill the iodine's unpleasant taste. In spite of their attempts to disinfect field water with iodine, some men still suffered from diarrhea and stomach cramps. It was part of life in the boonies.

Here along the high ridgelines, however, there was no place to collect water. Since their mission was to patrol the ridgelines in search of the enemy, going into jungle valleys to find water was out of the question. Having run out of water, each man resorted to draping his poncho across bushes at night in hopes of collecting enough dewfall to add to his canteen.

The stressors on the troops—carrying 50 pounds or so of gear through an enemy-infested tropical jungle while dressed in heavy fatigues, boots, and wearing a steel-pot helmet—were hard on any man. But doing all that without much water only added to the challenges of staying alive in the field.

At last, a resupply chopper came one afternoon bringing ammo, C-rations, and water. The water, in five-gallon cans, came off the chopper. The men formed about 10 lines, more or less by squads, one line for each can, and waited to fill their canteens. As the water was poured out, however, it became obvious it had been put into cans previously used for diesel fuel, making the water totally unfit to drink.

"This is shit! We can't drink this," said the first guy in line.

Not just one or two cans were contaminated. All were. They still had no potable water. The officers went up and down the lines, announcing the obvious...don't drink the water.

Virtually everyone in Delta Company was totally pissed. The general consensus was here they were out humping the boonies, risking their lives every day, and those rear-echelon dicks had only one job to do—send water—and they managed to royally screw that up.

"They're supposed to be supporting us, and they don't give a shit," Bill thought.

The men collected what little water they could from the dewfall that night. Those who had water shared with those who did not. The very next day, another resupply chopper brought potable water. Bill figured the Company Commander must have expressed to Battalion his extreme discouragement regarding the contaminated water, causing them to send out another chopper.

One afternoon Bill had gone with a new replacement to help him set out a trip flare, a process involving stringing a tight wire from the flare, and securing the wire to a bush. Anyone tripping over the wire causes the flare to ignite. Once ignited, the magnesium flare burns white hot, creating a pillar of fire about eight feet tall, which lasts maybe 30 seconds, causing a field of light to extend out from the flare about ten meters in all directions. While setting out the flare, the new guy got the wire too tight. When he went to pull his hand away, the flare ignited.

The flare had to be extinguished immediately. Otherwise, the dinks would know where they were. Troops are trained to cover an accidentally lit trip flare with their steel pot helmet.

"Smother it with your helmet," Bill told the new guy, who froze in place.

Bill quickly removed his own helmet, and covered the flare with it, using his foot to stomp his helmet into the ground. Try as he might to extinguish the flare, fire still shot out from under one side of the helmet, igniting Bill's pants leg from his ankle to his knee. Bill was too involved in putting out the flare to notice. His first indication that something was wrong was when he smelled meat burning.

Up to this point, he had felt no pain. Once he became aware of what was happening, he dropped his rifle, and starting slapping out the fire with his hands.

The new guy with him said "Damn, Boe, you caught on fire."

"Yeah, I did," Bill said, as he continued to beat out the flames.

Bill went immediately back to the hill.

"Good gosh, you gotta lot of burns," said Lieutenant Haas.

By this time, Bill's leg was blistered and pink. Doc Bowers, the medic, wanted him evacuated immediately. Haas got on the horn to the Captain, telling him Boe got burned by a trip flare, and needed to be evacuated.

The Captain said "We've got a resupply chopper coming in tomorrow. Bandage him up as best you can. We can't bring in a chopper now."

Lieutenant Haas told Bill what was going on. "You'll be going out on the resupply chopper tomorrow. You'll have to hump until then. They're not going to bring in a bird tonight to get you."

Doc Bowers wrapped Bill's leg in cellophane to keep air from getting to the wound, help prevent infection, and help stem the fluid loss that accompanies severe burns. Doc gave Bill some Darvon pills, and said "You gotta nasty burn. I can give you morphine if it's too painful."

Bill declined the morphine. The Darvon neutralized the pain, allowing him to sleep that night. The next morning, still on Darvon, he painlessly humped the hills with his burns. His pants leg from the knee down had been burned away. Only Doc's cellophane wrap protected his burned leg.

That afternoon, Doc Bowers affixed a medic's tag to Bill's collar. This was a paper tag resembling a postal tag which provided information as to the patient's unit, and his specific medical problems. The medic sending the man to the rear, authorized each tag by personally signing it. The medic's tag provided proper evidence a soldier needed medical care, and wasn't just shamming by hopping aboard a chopper to leave the field.

CHAPTER 29.
IN THE HOSPITAL AT KONTUM

Properly tagged, Bill boarded the resupply bird and flew to Kontum, where he was taken by Jeep to the hospital, a wooden structure with a tin roof.

He had not comprehended the severity of his injuries until he saw the faces of the doctors and nurses treating him. As they started an IV and cleaned and redressed his burns, someone told him he was lucky he wasn't going to lose his leg. While in the hospital, Bill was assigned to a long, narrow ward containing about 20 beds, 10 beds lined up on each side of the ward. A tag at the foot of his bed showed he was to be examined hourly due to the critical nature of his burns.

As did many soldiers, Bill used his time in the hospital to catch up on correspondence, and devour the available paperback books. Writing letters back home reminded him there was a place called "back home," and it was still there. He wrote to his mother, his brother Robert, to Robyn Ann Green, to Joanne Harris, and to Bruce Konrady, a long-time friend now in the Marine Corps. He got a letter and a care package from Wayne Boynton, a friend from back home. Wayne was now married and living at Ft. Benning, where he served as an Army Lieutenant. He also received a letter from a loyal pen pal, a sixth-grader from North Dakota. Bill was impressed that some kid he didn't know would take time to write him. Sending and receiving letters helped keep Bill oriented to life back in the world.

Before he had entered the hospital, several guys in Bill's platoon—Warren Conner, Shep Sheppard, and others—had expressed concerns about apparent but serious discrepancies in the way things were being run.

They had heard the weapons captured on LZ Hardcore were either traded, or sold on the black market. They knew such weapons should have been properly secured so as to not fall back into enemy hands.

Another huge concern was the way things had gone on LZ Mile High. Ordering a single, understrength platoon to set up a listening post by going out late in the afternoon into an NVA-infested jungle in which two companies had just been ambushed, and then expecting them to set up a decent perimeter before nightfall, with no entrenching tools, was sheer insanity.

Then not allowing them to recover for two days the bodies of their fellow soldiers killed in action, was unconscionable. Somebody, somewhere was relying too much on decisions made by officers looking at maps in some bunker 20 or so klicks away, when they should be listening more to their officers in the field with the troops.

There was also the issue of receiving contaminated water. Nobody who doesn't have his head up his ass puts drinking water in diesel-fuel cans. But that's what they got. With no water to drink, they could have lost men to dehydration and heat illnesses.

Finally, the Company had not been getting their sundry packs lately. These were large cardboard boxes normally delivered by resupply chopper every two weeks, containing cigarettes, candy, writing paper, ballpoint pens, soap, shaving cream, toothbrushes, disposable razors and other goodies people looked forward to receiving. There are few if any comforts in the field, and not receiving well-earned sundry packs was demoralizing. The rumor in the field was that some REMFs were selling Delta Company's sundry packs on the black market.

Bill was well aware of these situations, and shared their concerns.

Conner had said "Boe, you're a writer. You wrote for The Red and Black. You know how to put things in words. Can you write your Congressman, and tell him what's going on?"

Bill had agreed. So while here in the hospital, he wrote to Congressman Paul Rogers of West Palm Beach, expressing these concerns. Bill in essence told the Congressman his intention was to do the best he could to win the war, but they needed help because profiteers and others focused on self-gain were undermining the mission of the troops. Bill wrote about the Congressman's frequent trips to the Glades area, and how he'd often stop in to chat with his Uncle Olaf Boe, a civic-minded Rotarian who kept up with what was going on in the Glades.

Bill didn't know the Congressman's addresses, so he simply addressed his letter to "Paul Rogers, United States Congressman, West Palm Beach, Florida," put his U.S. Army return address in the upper left of the envelope, wrote FREE in the upper right-hand corner, and gave the letter to the medic who came by daily to pick up outgoing mail. Unsure the letter would even arrive at the Congressman's office, Bill didn't think about it much after that.

After a few days, his burns improved and he was discharged to further convalesce at the base camp, LZ Mary Lou. Although on the mend, he still wasn't well enough to return to the field.

He spent this time exploring, going out to look at the huge 175mm artillery positioned at Mary Lou. Their barrels looked to be 25-feet or so long, and he had heard they had a range of about 20 miles. The noise they made was deafening. Watching them fire was quite a show. Bill was impressed.

During this time, Bill found out from the Company Clerk, a guy named Carpenter, that he had been promoted to Sergeant E-5. It seemed those two NCO schools had paid off after all. Bill also learned from Carpenter that Delta Company had been sent to a firebase. To him that meant things were looking up. At least they were no longer alone in the boonies as they had been when he got burned.

As it turned out, however, things weren't looking up at all. Carpenter informed him that the Company had gotten mortared, two guys were killed, and half a dozen were wounded. At that point, it wasn't certain who had been killed. Bill could only speculate. Was it Lieutenant Haas? Who?

Later, when Carpenter learned the identity of the two KIAs, he informed Bill that they were Harff and Nelson.

William Henry Harff, Jr. from Kenosha, Wisconsin had been with Second Platoon for months now, at least since bridge guard days back in October. He was outside the bunker when a mortar landed and killed him outright. Harff was a quiet guy who kept mostly to himself. He wasn't an objectionable sort, just reserved. Bill recalled how Harff had meticulously kept a journal. Whenever he had a chance, he would be off by himself putting pen to paper. No one knew what Harff was writing. Was he writing about the war? Was he writing about what a bunch of jerks he was with? Was he writing poetry? Nobody knew. It used to bug Hollenbach to no end. "Why does he just sit over there and write?" Hollenbach would say. Now, Hollenbach and Harff were both gone. Maybe somewhere in the great beyond Hollenbach and Harff were finally talking over what Harff had penned. Nobody ever knew what happened to Harff's journal. All anyone ever knew was that it was important to him to write in it as often as he could.

Lewis Charles Nelson was from Seattle, a friendly handsome young guy with blonde hair and blue eyes. He was quiet and reserved, articulate and obviously well educated. Bill knew him more by sight than by interaction. Had he lived through the war, Bill imagined Nelson would have been a financial planner or maybe an engineer. Bill wasn't sure how Nelson ended up in Second Platoon. He remembered seeing him working with the mortar people back in January when they were on that hill southwest of Da Nang to contain the NVA, before Tet. As it turned out, Nelson's MOS was indeed 11C, mortars, and not 11B, which explained why he had been with the mortar guys. When manpower was low, the Army simply moved people around and put them wherever they decided. After all, every man is a rifleman, regardless of his MOS, by virtue of having completed Basic Combat Training. Cooks, for instance, were sometimes used as infantrymen in the field. Bill wondered if they had switched Nelson around, taking him out of the weapons platoon, and putting him in Second Platoon. The same mortar round that killed Harff also killed Nelson. As was the case with Harff, Nelson died outright.

Those wounded included Lonnie Leslie, the RTO, a gentile Southern boy who always did things right, Sergeant Archambo, and Warren Conner. Bill was stunned. He thought Tet might be the worst of things, but Tet was over and they were still racking up casualties. Since Tet, Bill had been out of the field for over a month, with the two NCO schools, and now with his burned leg. He felt pangs of guilt for not being in the field with his platoon.

Could he have made a difference? He'd never know.

The Company Clerk is a good man to know. He's often aware of what's going on since he types official orders, reports, and other documents the brass puts out. Carpenter was a good guy, supportive and efficient in his duties. From Carpenter, Bill learned of an opening for R&R in Australia.

"You've been in-country the longest," said Carpenter. "It's your choice to take it. You're senior man. Do you want it?"

Of course he wanted it. Bill had always wanted to go to Australia. His father had been in Australia during World War II, while serving as a Chief Petty Officer in the U.S. Coast Guard, and had told him stories from down under. Plus, it so happened there were Aussies stationed right here at LZ Mary Lou. They stood out, for sure. Their smart-looking bush hats with the upturned left brim, the not-quite-knee-length pants they wore, and their distinct Aussie accents set them apart from U.S. troops. The opening for an Australian R&R, the presence of Aussies—it all seemed as if the universe were telling Bill that Australia was soon to be in his future.

CHAPTER 30. R&R IN AUSTRALIA

Carpenter arranged for a week's R&R in Australia. He cut orders for Bill to board a C-130 flight to Cam Rahn Bay.

Before leaving, however, Bill had to go to the base clinic and be checked for venereal disease, since the Australians required one be VD-free before entering their country. Bill received a clean bill of health, and was issued a VD card, stating such.

He then retrieved his duffel bag and his AWOL bag from the base camp storage area. The AWOL bag was the name given to a type of black leather personal-items bag often available for purchase at most Post Exchanges. Bill had bought his while in Basic Training at Fort Benning. The base camp storage area was where most personal belongings were stored while men were in the field.

Bill didn't have much to pack. Into his AWOL bag, he put a pair of jeans, underwear, socks, and several film cartridges bought at the Kontum PX. While at the PX, he also purchased the brass, ribbons, and patches he was authorized to wear on the khaki uniform he'd travel in, including among others his 4th-Division patch, his Sergeant's chevrons, and his purple-heart ribbon. He knew these were the so-called dink ribbons—bought in Vietnam—and couldn't be used stateside because of a requirement that such items used in the States had to be purchased there. They were okay for overseas, however.

He also drew out of his account $400 in U.S. currency. Anything left when he got back would have to be exchanged for MPC.

He caught his C-130 flight to Cam Rahn Bay, where he showed his orders for Sydney R&R, and his VD card. After spending the night at the R&R transit barracks, at 0700 the next morning he reported to the terminal, ready to go, went through the gates, and later boarded a chartered Pan American flight filled with soldiers, all on the same Australian R&R trip.

While at Cam Rahn, he had met another guy from the 4th Division, originally from Estonia, who chose a Sydney R&R because there was a large community of Estonians there who had been displaced when the Soviets occupied Estonia after World War II. He and Bill decided to travel together, and share the expenses of accommodations.

Their flight took them first to Darwin, where the Aussies fumigated the plane, required the men to remove their boots before they got off the plane, and issued them slippers in the process. They hung around the Darwin airport a few hours due to some rule that all planes coming into Sydney had to come in during daylight. The robust White Swan beer served at the airport bar was certainly better than most of the brew they got in Vietnam. They finally took off again at a time that allowed them to arrive in Sydney as the sun was rising.

At Sydney, airport security personnel confiscated their boots, and checked their VD cards. Army buses picked them up and delivered them to the R&R Center, a military tourist center for U.S. Servicemen. Here, Bill rented a pair of shoes, slacks, and a couple of shirts. The U.S. Government prohibited troops from wearing their uniforms while in Australia to avoid any sight of drunk soldiers whoring around and disgracing the American military. Bill and his fellow soldiers were told exactly when to be back at the R&R Center at the end of their stay. They were duly informed that if any of them got arrested, or otherwise missed their flight back, they'd be in a world of shit.

The R&R Center arranged for lodging. The last thing Bill wanted was to stay where there were lots of soldiers. Wanting to interact with Australians, he avoided the typical soldier hotels in places such as Botany Bay, Kings Cross, and Bondi Beach. Instead, he and his buddy "Estonia" were assigned to a small flat in a building of flats at Manly Beach, away from the tourist crowd.

Catching a taxi to their flat, they arrived in the early evening. As they walked in the door, and went to the front desk, Bill noticed lots of beautiful, stylish young women in the lobby.

"We're happy to have you. I think you're going to like our accommodation," said the desk clerk. Bill was already tacitly agreeing with him.

"Who are all these girls?" Bill asked the clerk.

"These are Qantas stewardesses. Yes, Mister, I have a dream job here," he said.

Qantas airlines provided their stewardesses in training with a flat for a couple of weeks here until they could find their own housing in Sydney.

After checking in, Bill and Estonia went to a nearby restaurant for an inexpensive steak dinner, where they noticed Australian girls in miniskirts, which had come in vogue since Bill went to Vietnam. The sight of so many beautiful English-speaking girls displaying so much leg was truly remarkable. After dinner, they went back to their flat. Upstairs in the commons area of the building, they encountered some 30 drop-dead gorgeous girls who all got momentarily quiet when he and Estonia entered the room.

"You must be the boys from Vietnam," one of them said in a welcoming tone.

Bill and Estonia introduced themselves and after some brief chit-chat, one of the girls explained that they prepare their meals here every night, and would be most pleased to cook for two soldiers serving in Vietnam. They then asked Bill and Estonia if they had found a Sheila or a Judy. Neither of them understood the question, so the girls explained that a "Sheila" or a "Judy" were Aussie terms for… "interesting dates."

"May I have a word with you?" said one young lady to Bill. She had beautiful green eyes, and shoulder-length reddish auburn hair which flipped up at the ends. She introduced herself as Raelene Ansell from Adelaide. "I have a brother named Guy who's going to Vietnam," she said, adding "We have soldiers there too." She wanted to know what Vietnam would be like for her brother.

Bill told her about the Aussies he'd seen, and did his best to explain his idea of the Aussie mission in Vietnam. Their conversation led to an immediate, on-the-spot friendship.

"Bill, what do you intend to do tomorrow?" Raelene asked.

Bill said he wanted to see things authentically Australian—dingoes, a platypus, kangaroos, and so on. Raelene suggested he go to the Taronga Zoo, there in Sydney. He also said he wanted to see a rugby match, and attend a church while in Australia. Raelene was gracious enough to line everything up for him. While she went to her stewardess training every day, Bill saw the sights of Sydney. In the evenings, he and Raelene would go out together. They usually went to an outdoor café, enjoyed an evening meal, and conversed about their lives back home.

One morning Bill and Estonia went to a rugby game, a most violent sport with flesh hitting flesh, people getting splattered. All the players were big and muscular, resembling NFL linemen. Bill thought "This makes pro football look like a game of tiddly winks." There were no helmets or padding, and the object of the game is to get into an end zone but you can't have anyone blocking in front of you. Right before you get hit, you try to lateral the ball to a teammate behind you, who then has to survive as best he can. There are few timeouts. The game is ongoing mayhem and violence. Bill's impression was if they took those rugby players to the DMZ, the war would be won in a week.

One night, while Raelene was attending an evening class, Bill and Estonia went to the Whiskey-a-Go-Go in Sydney's Kings Cross. Bill had never seen Go-Go girls before. They sported short-cropped hair, miniskirts, and danced in an elevated cage. This whole Go-Go girl thing was a phenomenon that had apparently appeared while Bill was in Vietnam. There were no Go-Go girls in the boonies.

On one his outings with Raelene, he asked her about this new building construction project at the Sydney Harbor, which he had seen on the ferry headed to the Taronga Zoo. "Oh, that monstrosity," she said. "That's going to be the Sydney Opera House. Nobody likes it," she explained.

On the Sunday evening of his R&R, Bill attended an Anglican Church service, where he met a young man and his girlfriend. Following the service, Bill asked them to point out the Southern Cross. They did. They also drove him around, to show him the local sights. The young man's father held an important position with the Unilever Corporation which had a high-rise office building in Sydney offering perhaps the best view of the city. The young man told Bill to go to that building, and ask for his father, who would see to it Bill and his soldier friend were escorted to the top floor to enjoy the view.

Bill and Estonia did just that, and were graciously received once the staff determined the nature of their visit. As it turned out, the young man's father had been eagerly expecting them both. He personally took them to the building's roof for a spectacular look at Sydney. He then gave each of them a coupon for a fine meal in the company cafeteria, which they enjoyed immensely. After eating C-rations in so many muddy foxholes and bunkers, Bill was overwhelmed with gratitude at the very idea of enjoying a high-class free meal, and being treated royally by Australians in Sydney.

The Unilever exec had told Bill and Estonia to drop by his office before they left the building. Upon so doing, he gave each of them two large shopping bags filled with Unilever products—soaps, cosmetics, toothpaste, food items, and other goodies. That evening, since they could not take most of the products with them, or use them in Vietnam, Bill and Estonia gave their four bags of Unilever products to the Qantas girls, who were most grateful. One girl said "Do you realize each of these bags has about one hundred dollars' worth of merchandise which we need and can use?"

On his last night in Sydney, Bill had arranged for flowers to be sent to Raelene. It was his way of thanking her for her friendship and hospitality. Upon receiving them, she said "Bill, this is such a surprise. You never get flowers from an Australian man."

The next day, Bill and Estonia caught an early-morning taxi ride back to the R&R Center. They had leftover beer which they gave to the cabbie. Since there was plenty of time, the cabbie offered to tour them around. After explaining to the cabbie they didn't have a lot of money, the cabbie said "No, blokes, you're fighting a war. I'll give you a ride-around at no cost." He then took them on a 45-minute tour, after which he dropped them off, wished them safety and good luck, and told them it was an honor to have them in Australia.

At the R&R Center, they called roll, loaded the guys on Army buses, and took them to the airport. They boarded their Pan American return flight to Cam Rahn Bay. From Cam Rahn, Bill took connecting military flights back to Kontum, where he exchanged fifty dollars in U.S. currency for MPC, put away his duffel and his AWOL bag, changed back into his jungle fatigues, and checked out his rifle. Only a short time before, he was enjoying the sights of Sydney, and the companionship of Raelene. Now, he was back in the war, heading into God knows what.

CHAPTER 31. LZ BRILLO PAD

While in Kontum, one of the Lieutenants told Bill the letter he wrote to his Congressman was causing trouble, and he'd end up regretting he ever wrote it. At least, Bill thought, they're looking into it. Maybe some things would get fixed. The First Sergeant, whose nose was squarely out of joint likely due to the Congressional letter, had it out for Bill, and told him he'd better have his shit together and get his ass on the morning resupply chopper to rejoin Delta Company, now on LZ Brillo Pad, or he'd be AWOL.

"Top," said Bill, "the field is where I belong. I want to get back with my boys."

The next morning, 17 May, Bill showed up at the chopper pad in full field gear—ruck packed with C-rations, web gear, rifle, and a bandolier of ammo—and climbed aboard the first bird to Brillo Pad. During the 20-minute flight over mountains and dense jungle, the crew told Bill the hill was under constant mortar attack, so the landing would likely be hot.

As the bird set down, Bill jumped off and ran to the first bunker about 30 feet away. Inside Bill found six guys, introduced himself, explained he was newly back from R&R, and needed to find Second Platoon of Delta Company. The men told him they were in Charlie, 1st of the 12th, and that Delta, 1st of the 14th, was on the other side of the hill. "They got their side of the hill. We got ours," one of them said. Bill's only option was to run to Delta's side of the hill.

"When you go," one guy said, "run zig zag because they like to mortar this hill. Bill ran in serpentine fashion to his side of the hill. As he reached the hill's crest, he could see about 15 bunkers connected by trenches, and ducked into the closest bunker.

"I'm looking for Lieutenant Haas of Second Platoon," he told the guys inside.

"He's four bunkers down that way," one guy said.

Bill went hunkered down in the four-feet-deep trench leading to Haas's bunker. The Lieutenant welcomed Bill back, and since he was now a Sergeant, put him in charge of a bunker two bunkers down, which had five guys in it.

Bill learned that the previous night, the NVA had attacked and seized a permanent listening post near the perimeter, named "OP Hill," or "Hill 1124," as it was also called. A squad-sized group from Charlie Company 1st of the 12th which manned the OP had come under heavy attack, in which the dinks had even resorted to using flame throwers. A small contingent of men from Charlie, 1st of the 12th went to rescue them. That group's leader, Sergeant Anund Roark was killed when he heroically threw himself on a live grenade to save the lives of some of his men. All in all, two were killed and several wounded in the attack on OP Hill. Roark's bravery would earn him the Medal of Honor.

Later that day, Bill watched as two F-4 Phantom jets bombed OP Hill's bunker to ensure the NVA could not occupy it. As the F-4s would make their runs, drop their bombs, and begin to leave, Bill heard AK-47 ground fire coming from the OP Hill area. Having been on the receiving end of an F-4 during Tet, Bill thought it took a lot of guts for the dinks to remain there and shoot, especially since an AK is not at all likely to bring down a Phantom Jet.

That same day, talk of a KIA inside the perimeter during a mortar attack the day before reached Bill's bunker. Word was a mortar round had killed Private First Class Stephen Crawford while he was in his bunker. Bill remembered Crawford as a fresh young kid—he was only 18—who wanted to do everything right. He had been in-country for about three weeks when an NVA mortar round took his life. Bill heard that Crawford had been standing near the doorway of his bunker wearing a flak jacket when the round exploded just outside, in the trench. Apparently, Crawford's arm was raised, with his hand against the bunker's roof. Shrapnel hit him in the chest under the arm, where the jacket provided no protection.

That afternoon, incoming salvos of 15 to 20 rounds of 82-mm mortars began to pound the hill. While the rounds were falling, the only thing for the infantrymen to do was hunker down in their bunker next to the firing slats, and endure the attack. The artillery guys, on the other hand, remained outside in the artillery pits, largely exposed, as they returned fire to suspected NVA mortar positions. With sufficient moisture in the air, the artillery boys could sometimes see the path of enemy incoming rounds, and track those rounds to where they had been fired. Hunkered down in his bunker, Bill thought back over the mortar attacks he'd endured. Other than that so-called friendly mortar fire which killed Cheek Crosslin, and the Tet attacks, this was the only other time he had experienced incoming mortar rounds.

The attacks on LZ Brillo Pad turned out to be intense because this strategically placed firebase seriously thwarted the NVA's plans to take over South Vietnam. Brillo Pad was located about 28 klicks west of Kontum, as close as 30 klicks from the Cambodian border, and not far south of a network of logistical and supply passageways known collectively as the Ho Chi Minh trail. Brillo Pad's artillery pounded that notorious network with harassment and interdiction fire, termed H&I fire, meaning periodic fire on non-specific targets designed to screw with the enemy and hamper his efforts. Moreover, LZ Brillo Pad, along with LZs Roberts, Alamo, Bunker Hill, and Mile High were all firebases running nearly parallel to the Cambodian border, acting jointly as a blocking force for NVA infiltration toward Polei Kleng and Kontum.

When the Army first established LZ Brillo Pad earlier in the year, someone made the comment, "That's a rough place to put a firebase. The defenders of that hill will have to be as tough as Brillo Pads." The name stuck, and the soldiers defending it proved indeed to be every bit that tough.

The barren, high ridgeline now called LZ Brillo Pad had been cleared of jungle, with only scattered limbs and an occasional tree stump remaining atop bare earth. About 30 sandbagged bunkers dotting the hill sheltered troops from incoming fire. Low, circular walls of sandbags served as pits for artillery batteries. A single helipad on which the NVA had zeroed in their mortar tubes served the resupply and medevac choppers that came and went.

Bunkers on the hill were dug into the hillside. Most were about eight feet wide and 10 feet long, and roofed over with lumber or metal beams, sometimes reinforced with supporting metal planks, atop which sat plastic sheeting and three layers of sandbags. Inside a typical bunker were the firing slats—narrow, elongated openings about three feet long and nine inches high. Old wooden ammo boxes filled with dirt for ballast served as makeshift sills and provided a place to rest weapons when firing out. A two-feet-deep trench dug out of the earth below the firing slats allowed a man to stand while peering out of the slat. Earthen sleeping platforms about two feet high extended into the bunker's dirt walls. To avoid sleeping in the dirt, the men often covered these platforms with ponchos or sheets of cardboard from C-ration cases. Bunkers had an entranceway on each side to allow a quick exit.

Chest-deep trenches connected the bunkers, and allowed some protection if you crouched low. These trenches weren't just for going from one bunker to the next. They also served as exterior fighting positions, offering a 360-degree view. Brillo Pad's proximity to the Ho Chi Minh trail, and its artillery's ability to fire on that trail made it a prime target for being overrun, perhaps with a human-wave attack. In such an attack, remaining inside a bunker and firing out in only one direction would not be practical. Plus, the trenches offered a somewhat protective place from which to throw grenades when necessary.

That day, mortar fire continued to slam into the hill. If a chopper approached, the whole hill got peppered. The NVA obviously had forward observers watching the hill, and would respond to any type of movement by lobbing mortars. Orders were for the men to stay in their bunkers unless assigned some task which would cause them to venture out.

One such task was to participate in five-man reconnaissance patrols which would go out in the early morning beyond the perimeter wire, creep around the jungle looking for NVA or signs of NVA, then return close to dusk. As Squad Leader, Bill led four such patrols.

The men on patrol had no idea what they'd run into. For all they knew, a whole company of NVA could be waiting below in the jungle to annihilate them. For the safety and security of the firebase, however, they had to know what was going on outside the wire. That meant somebody had to go look. Other than what he went through at Tet, and that tragedy with the F-4 south of Hardcore, Bill found that leading these "suicide squads" as the men called them, were up to this point among the most nerve-wracking events of the war.

At first light the patrols made what they called "the wild run," meaning each man, one at a time, made a zig-zag dash over the 30-meter distance between the wire and the jungle. They knew NVA forward observers were watching all the while, and snipers could be in place, set to take any of them out. They ran one at a time so as not to bunch up. As one man disappeared into the jungle, they would wait about three minutes before the next man went. Those already in the jungle would act as security for those yet to make the run.

Besides the possibility of snipers hitting them on the wild run, the really big suspense was what might be waiting for them in the jungle. Would a platoon-size group of NVA allow the handful of men to enter the jungle, then overwhelm them with superior firepower? These mysteries weighed on Bill's mind, and on the minds of his companions.

Once in the jungle, the patrol would venture about 50 meters deeper into the jungle, find suitable concealment, hide, and observe. Their job was to be keenly aware of any possible sights or sounds of the enemy. They were not to make contact, just stealthily reconnoiter the area. "Hide and seek with M-16s" the men called it. The patrols traveled light so they could haul ass if they had to. They took no web gear or rucks. Besides water, they had only their rifles, ammo, and grenades. After about 30 minutes, they'd move another 50 meters or so, and once again, hide and observe. Every half hour, they'd use the Prick 25 to call in a sitrep back to the hill. At last light, they'd return to the hill, once again making the wild run, which was harder and even more daring this time because they had to run uphill to get back inside the wire.

That night, the hill was on full alert until about 2100 hours, when the men began to take one-hour turns on watch. The Army estimated there may have been an entire regiment of NVA surrounding the hill, and the possibility of a human-wave attack loomed large. To help ensure the dinks weren't creeping around outside the wire, those on watch were instructed to fire grenades every 10 minutes from their bloop guns into the jungle. Each of the 30 or so bunkers had at least one bloop gun and one or two crates of M-79 rounds for this purpose.

During his one-hour watch, Bill fired his six rounds at places he thought the dinks might approach. Having been in the jungle, he had a good idea where that would be.

The M-79 bloop gun could act as a mini-mortar. You could aim a round into the air, and have it drop anywhere you wanted if you were good at estimating distance. With practice, some guys got so accurate, they could often drop a grenade into an area the size of a hula hoop. Sometimes firing from the trench outside the bunker, Bill aimed his rounds to hit just beyond the wire. Those not on watch fell asleep in their bunker to the periodic blooping sounds of about 30 M-79s, followed by distant grenade explosions just outside the perimeter.

Noise discipline was in effect at night on the hill, meaning noise had to be kept to a minimum. During the daytime, however, in the absence of noise discipline the men were free to listen to their transistor radios. Actress and radio personality Chris Noel had a one-hour live show on AFVN out of Saigon each day. In the midst of this hellacious war, her sexy feminine voice was more than appealing to grubby GIs who could only dream of being near a woman. She made her shows personal, saying such things as "This song is for Charlie Company, somewhere out there on the border. You guys will be going home soon to your girls. Stay safe. And here's a kiss from Chris!" She would blow a kiss into the microphone…the only kiss the boys in the boonies would get anytime soon.

In contrast to Chris Noel each day, only once did Bill's radio pick up the infamous Hanoi Hannah, on Radio Hanoi. Hanoi Hannah was a Vietnamese who spoke English with a mild accent and played American songs on her radio propaganda show, the purpose of which was to undermine the morale of American troops. The Vietnam War's version of World War II's Tokyo Rose, Hanoi Hannah played popular American music, hoping to attract the listening ears of as many troops as possible. She'd play such songs as Bobby Vinton's "Mr. Lonely," or maybe "My Girl" by the Temptations, with the aim of creating a sense of melancholy and loneliness in young men far from home. Hanoi Hannah sometimes would mention the name of a specific American soldier, giving his unit and its exact location. She'd say such things as "Enjoy this music, GI, because your hill will be overrun and you'll be dead tomorrow." With these tactics, she intended to intimidate and frighten the troops. Particularly disturbing was the fact that Hanoi Hannah's details were often spot-on correct, highlighting the accuracy of North Vietnamese intelligence.

During the daytime, whenever the dinks detected movement on the hill, they'd fire mortar rounds in hopes of getting a kill. While the bunkers were the safest area, some things necessitated leaving your bunker—going to the water wagon, for instance. Or going to get C-rations, or more ammo. Those venturing out normally crept along the trench line, and would duck back into a bunker in the event of incoming fire. Using the latrines on the hill was a daring endeavor because anyone outside a bunker stood a higher chance of getting killed. At times, the men had no choice other than to urinate and defecate into a cardboard box or an empty sandbag inside the bunker.

One young soldier from North Carolina who shared Bill's bunker, totally fed up with the situation, announced he was going to the latrine. Toting his M-16 and a few squares of C-ration toilet paper, he ventured outside and jogged the 200 or so feet to the latrine. The dinks, obviously watching, waited for him to settle in. Then, from the valley below you could hear the "thwump, thwump" of mortar rounds leaving their tubes. The explosions of incoming rounds caused the young North Carolinian to run like a wounded possum straight to the bunker. Back inside and thoroughly pissed off, he said "I'm tired of shitting like a dog in the trench. Damned dinks won't even let you take a shit. This ain't right." One of the incoming rounds apparently damaged the latrine. Word came later over the radio "Gentlemen, don't be going to the shit house. I think that last round just blew out the crapper."

Later, Lieutenant Haas radioed Bill, and said "You need to come to my bunker. I need to talk to you." Bill went hunkered down in the trench and made his way to the Lieutenant, as ordered. "You wrote a letter to Congressman Paul Rogers," said Haas, who went on to say, "Apparently, Rogers was very efficient because your letter has had a tremendous impact. People in the company area are upset. You made some serious allegations. If what you said turns out to be true, there'll be some action taken. You're going out tomorrow to Pleiku, and the next day you'll testify. Then, as soon as they release you, you'll have to get back to the hill by the first available chopper."

The next day, 19 May, Bill, equipped with only his M-16 and a bandolier of ammo, climbed aboard an outgoing resupply chopper, headed to Pleiku. Arriving at around 1600 hours, he checked in at the company area, where he was told to go to his duffel bag, get his khakis, and shine his black shoes, the uniform he'd wear while testifying.

After retrieving his uniform, some Lieutenant unknown to Bill approached him and said "You're Sergeant Boe."

"Yes sir," Bill said.

"You'll be testifying. You're RA," the Lieutenant said, meaning Bill was Regular Army—that he had volunteered, and was not drafted. "You have pretty much screwed up your career."

"Sir," replied Bill, "I didn't enlist for a career. I enlisted because I wanted infantry. People are interfering with our mission to serve as well as we can."

"How do you know you're right?" said the Lieutenant.

"I'm confident, sir," said Bill. "Two machine guns we captured and turned in were never processed. Either they ended up as souvenirs for base camp commandos, or they were sold on the black market. Plus, there are complications with supply. I'm going to discuss these issues."

"You'll come out looking stupid," said the Lieutenant.

"I'll tell the truth and take that chance," said Bill.

"If the shit hits the fan back here, it will hit you, too," said the Lieutenant.

"That's okay. I've been through Tet and Brillo Pad. I can deal with shit," said Bill.

Not to be outdone, the arrogant asshole of a Lieutenant decided Bill needed saluting practice, and harassed him for a couple of hours in the hot sun, making him stand at attention and hold a salute.

The next morning, 20 May, after chow, the Company Clerk, Carpenter, told Bill he'd be taking him by jeep to the 4th Division Headquarters area, where he'd testify before the Inspector General. About half an hour later, Carpenter drove Bill to a Building that had "4th Division IG" over the door. There, Bill was ushered into the office of a Major. Upon seeing the Major, Bill saluted, and the Major returned his salute, after which he told Bill to be at ease. Having dispensed with these proper military courtesies, the Major invited Bill to sit in a chair in front of his desk, and offered Bill water.

Also in the Major's office was a Spec. 5 stenographer who would record exactly what Bill said. Before the proceedings began, Bill swore to "tell the truth, the whole truth, and nothing but the truth, so help me God."

"You are under oath," said the Major. "Anything you say that is intentionally false is perjury. I'm not here to intimidate you. I'm here to hear your story. You have several serious allegations. If we determine your testimony is accurate, if these allegations are true, some corrections will be made."

"I'm expressing concerns as I saw them, sir, and as other people told me," said Bill. "We had captured weapons, among which were two light Soviet machine guns, not processed by the chain of command. My belief is that a senior NCO either sold them as war souvenirs or sold them on the black market to the Vietnamese, which means they could fall back into the hands of the VC or the NVA, and be used to kill American troops."

"You have also expressed concerns that officers in the field weren't being listened to," said the Major.

Bill then related to him the incident at Mile High, including his concerns about sending fewer than 30 men to set up a listening post late in the afternoon with no entrenching tools, in an area where two companies had already recently been ambushed.

He continued to express his concerns about not being able to bring back the bodies. "The Army takes care of its own, sir. Those boys should have not have been left on that trail for two days, something which lowered the morale of the troops, making us feel expendable."

The Major explained to Bill that sometimes the higher Command has more info which causes them to make decisions not understood in the field. The job of those in the field is to follow orders, and not second guess commands.

They then discussed the diesel in the water delivered to them in the boonies. "How could anybody send contaminated water?" Bill asked rhetorically.

"That never should have happened," said the Major. "If it happened as you describe, that is not our procedure."

Bill then told the Major about not receiving the sundry packs. "Taxpayers have paid for them. We'd like to have them," he said. He went on to say "My sources said people in our supply department have been selling them on the black market. I've heard they get $200 for a sundry pack. That shouldn't happen," said Bill.

At the end of the half-hour interview, Bill told the Major he appreciated the time the Army had taken to look into these matters. The Major then told Bill there may be substantiation for his charges, and they'd be talking to a lot of people, but that he did not have to write his Congressman.

"The Army has a Chain of Command that could have handled these issues," said the Major.

"I wasn't aware of all that, sir. I was just trying to get some serious problems corrected."

Ending the interview, the Major said, "Sergeant Boe, I'll be looking at this and I'll debrief you in the morning."

Back in the company area, most people studiously avoided Bill since he was there to testify. The following day, 21 May, Carpenter drove Bill back to the IG's office. Bill met once again with the Major who told him "I've been investigating your concerns. There is basis to some of them. Others are telling me there are reasons they did what they did. Still, there have been some irregularities in what has occurred."

"Do I need to stay here and provide testimony, sir?" Bill asked

"No. You've done what you came here to do," replied the Major. Now I'm going to do what I have to do. You can return to your unit."

The next morning, 22 May, Bill dressed in his jungle fatigues, wolfed down morning chow, and with his rifle and bandolier of ammo, reported to the chopper pad. Within half an hour or so, he had caught a flight to Brillo Pad. Back on the LZ, he spoke with Lieutenant Haas who told him this was a serious investigation, and that much would come from it. "A lot is not going the way it should," said Haas, adding "Glad to have you back."

In Bill's absence, the NVA had mostly left the hill alone. Some guys guessed the dinks had run out of ammo. After all, NVA resupply likely came by truck or bicycle down the Ho Chi Minh trail, and maybe those supply lines weren't delivering. Or maybe the dinks went on to do something else.

Regardless of why the shelling had ceased, the absence of incoming fire allowed life on the hill to become more relaxed, and to take on a semblance of normalcy. Guys ventured outside to fortify their bunkers, visit friends in other bunkers, and to repair the latrine. With no incoming rounds, visits to the outhouse were now feasible. After relieving themselves in a bunker for the past few days, the men considered such visits a great luxury, a really big deal.

A journalist at heart, Bill wanted to document for posterity the goings-on at LZ Brillo Pad. He went about with his Kodak Instamatic to shoot photos of the hill, and the people on it.

After one of the resupply choppers had delivered its load, several guys came to Bill. "You won't believe what we got," one of them said. The chopper had delivered sundry packs for Delta Company. Bill had testified only a two days before, and suddenly the men are now receiving what they should have been getting all along—Hershey Tropical bars, various brands of cigarettes, other candies, tooth brushes, real stateside toothpaste, and other items most welcomed in the boonies. Things were looking up.

The next morning, 23 May, Father Hagen came on a resupply chopper to visit. Although he was technically the Battalion chaplain for the 1st of the 14th, the good priest also ministered to those in the 1st of the 12th, to the artillery guys, and indeed to everyone on the hill. He brought with him his spiked egg nog, and gave away New Testaments to anyone who wanted one. He inquired if anyone had family issues or other problems he could help with. He went from bunker to bunker praying with the men, "Father, bless these boys. Put your hand around them, embrace them with your love." He offered communion to anyone who wanted it. After a couple of hours, Father Hagen, now an icon among chaplains for his willingness to come to the field, left on a resupply chopper.

On 24 May at 1900 hours, rounds from recoilless rifles slammed into the perimeter, marking the beginning of a four-day siege of the hill. During this time, the boys of Brillo Pad caught pure hell, enduring not only recoilless rifle fire, but also 82 mm mortars, B-40 rockets, and 122 mm rockets.

The dinks badly wanted this hill, and were throwing everything in their · arsenal at it in hopes of eventually overrunning it.

In the relative protection of his bunker, Bill reflected over his time in combat, comparing the danger from both mortars and small-arms fire. Mortars wreaked more havoc than small arms, he thought. What he especially hated about mortar rounds was you can't hear them, and you normally can't see them either. They don't whistle. They don't whoosh. Nothing. Unless you can manage to track one by the slight trail it sometimes leaves in moist air, you have no idea where it's about to hit. But once you hear the "thwump" as an NVA mortar round leaves its tube from the jungled valley below, you know it's coming your way. Where will it land? In his bunker Bill thought of the old saying "I shot an arrow into the air. It fell to earth I know not where."

During the siege, the five-man recon patrols still went out. On the morning of 26 May, Bill led a patrol beyond the perimeter and into the jungle in the midst of a heavy mortar and rocket attack. As the mortar rounds fell, six-foot long Soviet-made 122 mm rockets weighing more than 100 pounds also whizzed in to deliver their powerful 15-pound payload of explosives. Fired from possibly three to 11 kilometers away, 122s came in at an angle, having a rising and falling trajectory. The guys called them "flying fence posts," because that's what they looked like. These rockets were perhaps the most powerful weapon the NVA used on Brillo Pad during the siege. With so many rounds hitting the hill, Bill felt safer leading his recon patrol into the enemy territory of the jungle, than remaining on the firebase.

On his recon patrols, Bill had developed the technique of putting out trip flares across heavily used trails. If the dinks tripped a flare, the boys on the hill could call in mortar fire, or hit the location with M-79 bloop guns. Or they could even call in "Spooky," also known as "Puff the Magic Dragon." This was a C-47 modified by attaching three six-barrel mini-guns which fired out of the pilot's side of the aircraft. Puff's firepower was overwhelming. By circling the targeted area, and rolling 30 degrees to port, the plane could aim and fire its three 7.62 mm guns, which could put out one bullet per square foot, covering the area of a football field. The dinks were totally intimidated by Spooky. They dared not fire at Spooky with an AK-47. They might have used an anti-aircraft gun if they had it, but not small arms. Knowing the danger they faced from ground attack, the boys of Brillo loved to see Spooky make its runs around the hill.

Besides the trip flares, Bill's patrol once set out a booby trap, consisting of a C-ration can with a grenade placed inside. To the pin, they attached a trip wire. The idea was anyone tripping the wire would cause the pin to be pulled, the grenade to exit the can, and the spoon to drop off. After five to seven seconds, the grenade would explode. They did hear the grenade explode one night, meaning it likely accomplished its purpose. Since their own guys would be creeping around the jungle, however, they decided not to set more booby traps in case they got one of their own men.

Sitting in the jungle on this day, Bill's recon patrol found itself in the crossfire of a mortar fight. NVA mortars would pass overhead on their way to the hill, and mortars from the hill would fly over on their way to the dinks. Those in the patrol sometimes held their breath, hoping no mortar would hit where they were. Bill plotted the direction of incoming rounds in case that information proved useful in carrying out artillery and air strikes.

At day's end the patrol made its way back to the jungle's edge by the hill. Bill used the radio to alert the CP that his patrol was returning to the perimeter. "We'll be running like hell to get back inside the wire, so don't light us up," Bill said. He went on to request fire support from the trenches if they came under enemy attack. As always, the wild run back inside the wire was harder and scarier on the return trip because of the uphill run.

Later that day, 26 May, Bill learned that Sergeant Hughes, the Platoon Sergeant, had been wounded by shrapnel and medevacked out. Lieutenant Haas made Bill the Platoon Sergeant, and he moved his ruck sack into the CP with Haas, the medic, and the RTO.

That same day, a couple of 82 mm mortars hit two bunkers to Bill's right. The first round shook the bunker. The second blew off part of the roof, burying the men in sandbags. In that bunker were Frank Belcher, M-60 machine gunner, his assistant gunner, Arnold Lovelace, and ammo bearer Stephen Forgey.

"Oh, God," Bill thought, "those boys are all dead." A few minutes later, after hurriedly digging themselves out, Bill saw all three piling out of the now-destroyed bunker and into the bunker next to him, shared by Roy Winter, Bill Boetje, and George Billups. The incoming rounds did not let up.

Grabbing his M-16 and a bandolier, Bill ran to the next bunker to see about those hit by the mortar. Once inside, he saw the three men, shaken but not apparently wounded.

"Is anyone left in that bunker?" he asked.

"No, we're all here," said Belcher.

"Is anyone wounded?" asked Bill.

"No," replied Belcher.

"Did you get your weapons out?" asked Bill.

"No, we left the M-60 in there," said Belcher. "We didn't have time to get it. We were afraid the next round would come right through the hole in the roof, blowing us to bits."

"We're going to need that machine gun. I'll go get it," said Bill.

Bill ran outside, down the trench line, and into the partially roofless bunker, where he found the machine gun near the firing port. Examining it, he found it to be fully functional. Just then, a powerful, shoulder-fired B-40 rocket slammed into the lower front of the already-damaged bunker. Dink forward observers had obviously seen Bill go in the bunker, and were now intent on killing him. The explosion, which sounded to Bill like a couple of cherry bombs going off right next to him, caused the bunker to shake. Sand from ripped-open sandbags sifted down.

"Are you okay, Boe?" yelled someone from the next bunker.

"Yeah, I'm fine," Bill yelled back.

Just then, Bill heard the sho-o-o-om-boom sound of another incoming rocket as it passed over the bunker's right front corner. About 20 seconds later, a third rocket impacted right below the front of the bunker.

At that point, Bill knew the dinks had heard him. He was their target. "I'm shutting up," he thought. "Maybe the dinks will think they got me."

As he hunkered down in the remains of the bunker anticipating more incoming rockets, he knew these could be his last moments. Then, amidst the rubble, he saw a can of C-ration pears, a highly prized treat in the field. "If I'm going to die, I'm going to at least have pears for my last supper," he thought. With his P-38 can opener, he opened the can and scarfed down the pears. Ever the journalist, and wanting to document this event, he then used his Kodak Instamatic to photograph the gaping hole in the top of the bunker.

No more rockets were fired at him. After about ten minutes, Bill dashed down the trench line into the next bunker with Belcher's M-60 and his own M-16 slung over his back. Once again, he confirmed all were okay. Giving Belcher his machine gun, he told him "We'll get you more ammo tomorrow. We might need this firepower. We gotta have this gun operational."

Belcher and Lovelace started disassembling the gun to make sure all its parts looked okay, and that when reassembled it would still work. Bill returned to his bunker and contacted Lieutenant Haas on the radio. Referring to the damaged bunker, Bill told Haas "We have a bunker knocked out now that's not in condition to defend the hill, and a blind spot on the perimeter." He also told Haas there were no casualties.

Sometime later, Bill heard through the Brillo Pad bunker-to-bunker grapevine that a soldier had been shot the day before with an M-79 grenade launcher, and the high-explosive round had penetrated his leg. The actual details of the incident were that Sam Agius, a Second-Platoon grenadier from Michigan, was sitting on a five-gallon can in his bunker under the firing slat when another of the platoon's grenadiers accidentally shot him in the left leg. This other grenadier had been on a recon patrol which had just exchanged fire with dinks outside the wire, and headed back into the perimeter. Mortar rounds hit the hill as the grenadier approached Sam's bunker. "Get in the bunker!" those inside yelled. Entering the bunker involved a step down. As the returning grenadier went to take that step, what was likely a sympathetic trigger squeeze, an involuntary reflex action of sorts, caused the gun to fire, creating a cloud of dust inside the bunker. The egg-size projectile hit Sam in the calf, twisted into and through his pants leg, buried itself about an inch deep into his flesh, and came to rest on a bone. The round's impact spun Sam around and he fell face down on the ground. As a safety feature, M-79 grenade rounds are designed to arm themselves only after they have traveled 30 meters. That's the idea, anyway, but they don't always work like that. Fortunately, for everyone involved, the round in this case performed exactly as designed. Sam lay on the ground in the dust-filled bunker with a live grenade in his lower leg.

Bill Boetje, his good buddy, immediately jumped on Sam to help him compose himself. "Don't touch it," said Boetje. "It's a live round." Sam cringed at the thought of what was happening. Soon, two men, cleaner than most of the grunts, and probably from the medic group at the top of the hill, came to provide medical aid. One was a Major, maybe a doctor, and the other a medic. They gave Sam morphine, and told Boetje to go find a can. The two seemed to know exactly what they were doing. They worked to dislodge the round from Sam's leg, while incoming mortars constantly exploded outside. After snipping away some of Sam's flesh, they finally extracted the round from his leg, put it in the can Boetje had brought, took it outside, and threw it out of the perimeter. It exploded on impact. Despite having difficulty landing because of enemy fire, a chopper medevacked Sam out that night.

Bill had never before heard of anyone having a live grenade buried in his leg. Indeed, the whole incident soon sparked lots of conversation among the men on LZ Brillo Pad.

One afternoon on the hill at about 1400 hours, the men were in their bunkers listening to AFVN radio, while mortar rounds fell outside.

The playing of radios was permitted during daylight hours because there was no need for noise discipline to conceal positions. The enemy already knew where the troops were since he could see them from the jungle. "The Letter," by the Box Tops was perhaps the most popular song in Vietnam at this time, and a great sing-along. While the mortar rounds fell, the sounds of wanting a ticket for an aeroplane, with no time for a fast train came from multiple transistor radios in the 15 bunkers on Delta Company's side of the hill. Somewhere in the middle of the bunker line, guys from one of the bunkers starting singing along to the radio. Those next to them joined in. The singing spread rapidly from bunker to bunker until that whole side of the hill sang in unison, each bunker trying to outperform the next, all the while being mortared. Some 60 or so young Americans were all singing "The Letter," during the attack. The spontaneous sing-along would have made Mitch Miller proud, and surely screwed with the dinks whose mortar fire created a GI song fest.

Around 2100 hours on 27 May Bill was in a bunker with Boetje and Sheppard when suddenly heavy machine-gun fire ripped into the bunker's walls. The front of the bunker seemed to explode from the inside. Rounds were ripping through sandbags along the front of the bunker and then hitting the metal rods on the bunker's roof. The dinks had zeroed in on them, with what the men recognized as .51 caliber anti-aircraft fire from the valley below, coming in at an angle. The heavy machine-gun firing lasted a full three to four minutes. Those inside were confused and terrorized that bullets were disintegrating their bunker. They pushed each other outside and got low in the trench. With the massive amounts of incoming fire power, nobody dared stick his head above the trench to return fire. That would have been a good way to get it shot off by an anti-aircraft gun.

The next day, 28 May, Boetje and Bill salvaged .51 caliber rounds from the bunker's sandbags, confirming they had indeed been hit with anti-aircraft fire. The dinks were bringing out the big guns. They wanted this hill. They wanted it badly. Somebody said 19 May had been Ho Chi Minh's birthday, and they wanted the hill as a present for him.

That day, 82 mm mortar rounds started hitting between the bunkers and the perimeter wire. Boetje commented "It looks like the B-string has arrived."

"There is no B-sting," Bill said. "They're blowing out our Claymore lines. I think they want to come up our side of the hill."

The mortar barrage near the perimeter had severed the Claymore lines, convincing Bill the dinks were preparing to attack that night from that location. At that very spot, a two-to-three-feet-deep gully ran from the bunker and fanned out to the concertina wire below, creating a blind spot. That evening, around dusk, Bill slipped into the gulley, where he strategically placed trip flares and three Claymore mines, one in the back of the gully, one on the floor of the gulley, and one just inside the concertina wire. Bill instructed his team that if any trip flares were ignited to detonate all three mines. "I think we're going to have visitors tonight," he said.

That night, recoilless rifle fire and mortars slammed into the hill. Other incoming fire hit near the bunkers. Those in Bill's bunker crouched low, especially as rockets went flying by. Later, with Sheppard on watch and peering out of the firing slat, the trip flares went off. "Dinks in the wire!" he yelled, and detonated all three Claymores. Everyone surged out of their bunkers, and from the trenches began to throw grenades, or fire M-79s and M-16s at the spot where the dinks had entered the perimeter.

In the reddish glow of the trip flares, Bill saw figures moving, and fired at them with his M-16. "For once," he thought, "my M-16 actually works when I need it to." From below, you could hear numerous dink sappers screaming and moaning. The whole sapper attack lasted 10 to 15 minutes. The hill remained on full alert the rest of the night.

The following morning, 29 May, Lieutenant Haas sent out a patrol led by Sergeant Michaels to examine the area by the wire and beyond. Michaels and his men discovered a gap cut into the wire. Still hanging in the wire was an undetonated Bangalore torpedo. They also found NVA pith helmets with brains in them, B-40 rockets, AK-47s, and two sandbags filled with Chi-com grenades. Apparently, once inside the wire, the dinks were planning to go from bunker to bunker, and toss grenades into them.

At around 1000 hours, the Major on the hill came to congratulate the men for stopping the attack. "Looks like their intent was to get into the trench line, and blow up the bunkers," he said. The Major also said that based on an inventory medics took of body parts, there were at least eight dead dinks, with probably at least another dozen which couldn't be confirmed. Bill's bunker was credited for the eight confirmed kills.

Lieutenant Haas told the Major that Sergeant Boe had suspected the attack, which is why Boe had put out more Claymores the night before. The Major congratulated Haas and his men on a job well done.

The NVA were obviously intent on throwing everything they had at LZ Brillo Pad in hopes of overrunning it. Around 1200 hours orders came over the radio for everyone on the hill to seal themselves inside their bunkers with sandbags. They were to seal up doors and slats, so no flying shrapnel could come in. They were to get down low inside the bunkers, and not look outside. As ordered the men spent much of the afternoon filling sandbags with their steel pots, and sealing the bunkers.

The reason for the unusual orders was because later in the day, there'd be a special bombing run in which cluster bomb units, or CBUs as they're called, would saturate the jungle near the hill with flying shrapnel. CBUs are special bombs that once dropped, break into numerous sub-munitions similar in this case to hundreds of mini hand grenades, which would scatter shrapnel everywhere, with the intent of killing anyone in the target area. If the dinks thought they were going to amass troops near the hill for a human-wave attack, they had another think coming.

Later that day, with everyone safely inside a bunker, jets flew over the hill. Each time they made a run and dropped their payload, it sounded to Bill like the most active Fourth of July he'd ever heard, with what seemed to be massive strings of Black Cat firecrackers popping off all around outside. After about 10 to 15 seconds, the popping would cease, that is until another jet made another run, and then the popping would start all over again. The jets made about three runs and left. A few minutes later, Bill heard over the radio the bombings were completed, and they could go outside. The men were instructed to look out for undetonated munitions, which would be round and look similar to ping-pong balls or tennis balls. Anyone encountering these munitions were to mark them, so the engineers could come in and destroy them in place.

For a couple of afternoons during the seige, Skyraiders, single engine prop-driven planes looking like something straight out of World War II, came to bomb and strafe the nearby jungle. In the process, they put on quite an air show for the troops on the hill. As they'd come in to make their runs, they'd dip their wings to those on Brillo Pad. They came in low and slow so you could clearly see the faces of the pilots. Bill saw one of the pilots who sported a mustache, acknowledge the men on the ground with a big grin. The guys loved the Skyraiders. The dinks were intent on overrunning and annihilating everyone on the hill, and they knew the Skyraiders were helping make sure that didn't happen.

To continue to counteract the NVA, word came there'd be an Arc Light attack on an area near the hill. Operation Arc Light involved the use of B-52 bombers, which would drop huge bombs weighing perhaps 500 or 750 pounds. The men were informed that the bombs would hit as close as possible to the hill without undue danger to those on it. They were ordered to be in the bunkers during the attack. The idea was to massively destroy NVA forces surrounding the hill.

Bill never saw or even heard the B-52s. They fly high—out of sight and earshot. But he did hear the rolling thunder of trails of bombs as they smashed into the jungle as close as a klick away. He saw the night sky briefly light up almost as if it were daylight. "Maybe the dinks will hightail it back to Cambodia," he hoped. "At least those who can survive that mass of bombs."

On this day, Bravo Company had been brought in to relieve Delta. That night the men shared the bunkers. Delta had been on that hill for three weeks, and deserved a break. Lieutenant Bender, the Company

Commander, would be leading them in the early morning hours through the jungle down the hill's southwest slope and on to some new location.

Before leaving, Bill talked with some of the artillery boys who kept up with battlefield statistics. The Americans had 17 people killed on and around Brillo Pad, and about 40 wounded.

The next morning, as the company led by Lieutenant Bender quietly made its way in the pre-dawn darkness down the jungled slope of LZ Brillo Pad, Bill and the others were more than ready to say good-bye to the hill the NVA wanted but could never take.

An iconic photo of LZ Brillo Pad

Bill pulls .51 caliber slugs out of his bunker on LZ Brillo Pad.

Captured enemy weaponry the morning after the NVA invaded the perimeter.
From left to right -- Lindsey, Billups, Phillips, SGT Michaels

Sky Raiders attack NVA on OP Hill.

Bill Boetje on LZ Brillo Pad. Photo courtesy of Sam Agius.

Sam Agius holds his bloop gun as Bill Boetje looks on.
Photo courtesy of Sam Agius.

CHAPTER 32. AMBUSHED

The trek away from Brillo Pad took them down the side of the hill, and into the open where they rode on top of armored personnel carriers for three or four klicks. The ride led them down jungle trails, but Bill noticed there weren't many big hardwood trees like the ones near LZ Mile High. The fact they were riding on APCs seemed to indicate an apparent absence of NVA, which surprised Bill, especially after what they had experienced on LZ Mile High and LZ Brillo Pad. Hopping off the APCs after their short ride, the men of Delta Company humped uphill about 20 minutes before arriving at the relatively low hilltop spot which would be their new home for a while.

Lieutenant Bender selected a good landing zone, and the men began to clear the hilltop of bamboo and other jungle foliage. They also did what they could to secure the area. They set up a company CP, dug shallow fox holes, and established a company perimeter. The next few days on LZ Bingo were quiet, a refreshing change from the hellacious incoming fire back on Brillo Pad.

A few days after arriving on Bingo, Bill Boetje heard on his transistor radio that Bobby Kennedy and been shot. "Good God," said Boetje, "they killed another Kennedy. They shot Bobby Kennedy. We're safer here in Vietnam than it is for the Kennedys back home." Boetje had his own way of saying things. He also had a good sense of humor, which served to lighten the mental load of the men around him. At only 19, he was the Platoon's stand-up comedian. The morning after the dinks got in the wire on LZ Brillo Pad, the men were told to "look around your position to see if they're any duds up there," meaning unexploded mortar rounds, B-40 rockets, and so on. Boetje said "What? Did we get new replacements?" He could imitate people quite well, and was especially good at imitating Lyndon Johnson. Boetje made people laugh when there wasn't much to laugh about.

Boetje was from Rock Island, Illinois, where his family owned a company producing specialized, tasty mustard. The Boetjes back home kept Second Platoon well supplied with their product. Everyone loved Boetje mustard because it made the C-rations more palatable.

About this time Lieutenant Bender had received word that LRRP patrols had found evidence of light enemy use of a trail near Bingo. Battalion wanted to know what the NVA were up to, and figured an NVA prisoner might provide the information they needed. Consequently, Lieutenant Bender ordered Second Platoon to set up an ambush at a site about half a klick away from Bingo where the LRRPs had found evidence of enemy movement. The idea was to try to capture a prisoner. They were to shoot one in the legs if necessary. Whoever was directly responsible for bringing in a prisoner would receive a week's in-country R&R.

After a C-ration breakfast, on the morning of 7 June, Second Platoon led by Lieutenant Haas, with Bill second in command, moved out to accomplish their mission. Bill liked Haas, who with his heavy sturdy glasses and dark wavy hair looked more like a young college professor than an infantry officer. Haas did a great job in the field. He could read maps expertly, and lead men under difficult conditions. He was a fine officer, always looking out for those in his charge. During his time in the field with Lieutenant Haas, Bill had developed a great respect for the man, and a trust in his judgment. He was proud to serve with him.

Bill was among the 30 men leaving the hill that morning. The others included Lieutenant Jim Haas, John Sheppard, Penland, Phillips, Dennis Christensen, William Boone, Frank Belcher, Eddie Bolton, Arnold Lovelace, Stephen Forgey, Dennis Mikulenka, Bridges, Ronda, Lindsey, Roy Winter, Julio Serrano-Rivera, Billups, Wuhrman, Ezzel, Bill Boetje, Ford, Robles, Wilson, Manuel, Michaels, Davis, Ferguson, Richards and Leroy Orth.

Since they were to be out possibly as long as three days, and would not be resupplied, everyone carried extra ammo and grenades, plus sufficient C-rations and several canteens of water. They didn't know it then, but those extra munitions would soon work to their advantage.

Having left the perimeter some 15 minutes earlier, Second Platoon maintained a distance of 10 or so feet between each man as they followed a trail along the crest of a ridge. As is the case with all ridges, the terrain sloped down on either side of the crest.

Dennis Mikulenka walked point. A rifleman followed him, then came a grenadier. Next in line was Frank Belcher's M-60 gun team. Typical of a gun team, an ammo bearer walked in front, then came the Belcher the gunner, followed by Arnold Lovelace the assistant gunner, and Stephen Forgey the other ammo bearer. Then came Lieutenant Haas, Phillips his RTO, and Doc Christensen the Platoon Medic. They were followed in the line by a number of riflemen. Then came Sergeant Boe, along with John Sheppard his RTO. Eddie Bolton's M-60 gun team followed Boe and Sheppard, with an ammo bearer up front, followed by Bolton the gunner, then the assistant gunner and another ammo bearer. Last in line were a grenadier and a rifleman, the latter acting as the Platoon's drag security.

About 400 meters out of Bingo, Mikulenka made a fateful decision which likely saved almost the entire Platoon. Instead of staying on the trail, he decided to lead the platoon off trail to the left, down the slope a bit, about 20 feet into the jungle. They could still see and follow the trail to their right. But now they weren't exposing themselves by walking on it. Two or three minutes later, Mikunlenka saw an NVA soldier on the trail some 20 feet away standing up and looking around. Mikulenka shot him.

Everybody hit the dirt. Lieutenant Haas got on the horn to Bill. "I think our point man just shot an NVA scout," said Haas. "Take two men, go up there, recover the weapon, and search the body to see if there are documents or information on it." The Platoon's mission had been to gather information regarding NVA activity. Only a few minutes out of Bingo, the hope was they'd found what they were looking for. As Bill headed up to

Mikulenka, all hell broke loose. A wall of rifle fire erupted from the direction of the trail.

If Second Platoon had been on that trail, they would have walked directly into the jaws of an NVA ambush, and been massacred. Maybe the NVA were trying to recreate the success they had ambushing Americans at LZ Mile High back on 15 April. Or maybe they got tired of getting their asses kicked at LZ Brillo Pad, and turned to an easier target. Whatever the reason, the plan was to hit the Americans as they left the hill, and followed the trail. The plan would have worked, had not Mikulenka led the Platoon off trail.

The element of surprise is all important in an ambush. The lead elements of Second Platoon may have walked into the ambush's killing zone when Mikulenka veered from the trail. Then when Mikulenka fired the first shot, it alerted his platoon to take cover. Since they were now on the ground and down the slope a bit, the ridge's crest between Second Platoon and the NVA provided cover from the enemy's rifle fire, which, for the most part, zipped by over their heads. Moreover, the NVA probably didn't know where their prey had gone since the Platoon was no longer on the trail, as expected. And the NVA likely didn't know how many GIs they were up against. Such uncertainty on the enemy's part surely worked to Second Platoon's advantage.

Bill knew at this point their only hope was to keep up a massive wall of rifle fire. He knew firepower was all important in a firefight. A continuous wall of fire would stop a possibly large NVA force from charging across the trail, and straight into Second Platoon. To better see and to cover the trail, they had to crawl up a few feet to much nearer the top of the slope, exposing themselves more to enemy fire. Although most of the guys couldn't see a target, they laid down a wall of fire up and down the trail by shooting three- and four-round bursts with M-16s.

As Bill lay on the ground firing, a Chi-com grenade flew over his shoulder, and landed about 10 feet behind him, on the other side of some foliage. It lay there sparking from the fuse in the handle. Bill thought for a nanosecond about throwing it back, but rejected that idea because he didn't know how long it would take the grenade to detonate. He immediately low-crawled away from it. Just then, he heard the explosion. It felt as if someone had slugged him in his right buttock and lower back. He put his hand back there, and it came back covered with blood. He knew he was hit, but had to stay in the fight.

"The sons-of-bitches are throwing grenades," he thought. He scrambled low, working his way up and down the firing line, telling his men to keep firing and to throw grenades. A grenade could kill someone on the other side of the ridge, while bullets likely passed right over the enemy. Whatever they did, Bill knew they had to maintain their fire power if they hoped to keep the dinks from assaulting across the trail and into their faces.

Bill was also worried the dinks might turn the flanks and come in from behind the Platoon. If that happened, Second Platoon would be screwed. To try to prevent it, Bill scrambled to his right, running hunched over, heading toward the right flank. Passing Bolton's gun team, he saw Bolton saturating the jungle with lethal fire. He continued on to the right flank where Boetje, Winter, and Rivera were hunkered down and firing across the trail. The trailed curved there, and the three could see 50 feet down the trail beyond where the fighting was taking place. "Don't let them cross the trail to your right," Bill told them. And they didn't. Before the firefight was over, Boetje had killed one NVA. Rivera had killed one. And another was down. Among them they had killed three NVA soldiers whose bodies now littered the trail. Another half dozen enemy soldiers came up, saw the bodies, and retreated back down their side of the slope.

After leaving Boetje, Winter, and Rivera, Bill went back toward the left flank. As he passed Bolton and his team, still clattering away with the M-60, he came upon Billups who had frag wounds in his arm.

"Sarge, I've been hit," Billups said.

"We've all been hit," said Bill, as he used Billups's own bandage to wrap the wounded arm. "I need you need to get up to that firing line and start shooting that M-79. Make noise. We can't have those boys coming across that trail into our faces."

After patching up Billups, Bill continued back up the firing line toward the left flank, passing riflemen shooting, changing magazines, and shooting some more. Many of the guys had only recently come to the field. This was their first firefight, and they were performing exactly as they were trained to do. Lindsey was hit but still firing. Bill was proud of them. He suspected their Drill Sergeants would have been proud of them too.

During the firefight, a dozen or more B-40 rockets whizzed by over-head, each leaving a characteristic trail of sparks. Although the sight of the flying rockets was intimidating, they inflicted no damage. Bill knew that B-40s were designed to take out stationary targets such as vehicles and bunkers. Why the NVA were firing them indiscriminately at troops they couldn't even see, he didn't know. Maybe things got chaotic for them and they weren't thinking straight after their ambush trap was foiled.

Besides the rockets, there were explosions overhead. Bill suspected the dinks were shooting mortars at them, and the rounds were blowing up when they hit the treetops, raining down shrapnel.

Bill scrambled to the front where Belcher's lead gun team was firing up and down the trail with the M-60. At that location, the trail curved to the left. Bill instructed four riflemen to post themselves about five feet apart down the slope, effectively creating a left-flank perimeter. "Look out in front of you. If they cross that trail and try to come in behind us, you guys are going to stop them," said Bill.

Bill then went back to the firing line, between the two machine guns. He had fired two magazines when he saw movement in the bushes at the base of a tree about 30 feet away. "I'm going to throw a grenade," he said to himself, as his thoughts flashbacked to Little League tryouts, in which he wasn't that great at throwing the ball. Still, he grabbed a grenade from his belt, pulled the pin, and let it fly. It hit a tree, and bounced back toward him, exploding nearby in the trail.

Ronda, who had frequently touted his skills as a baseball player, was off to Bill's right, down the slope a bit, changing magazines. "Ronda," Bill said. "Get up here. I want you to be a baseball pitcher." Ronda scrambled up to where Bill was.

"Throw a grenade on the right-hand side of that tree. There's a gook moving around in the bushes there. I threw one and about killed myself. Can you throw a hard ball right at the base of that tree. That's the plate."

"I can put it anywhere I want," said Ronda.

Ronda hurled it right where Bill had directed, just like a pro ball player would. The explosion made limbs and other vegetation fly in the air. Screaming and yelling came from the other side of the trail.

Bill looked down the trail to the left where he saw more movement in the foliage.

"I'm going to point my rifle," he told Ronda. "I want you to put a grenade right on them." Ronda threw the grenade across the trail. It hit right in the clump of bushes where Bill had pointed. There were more screams.

"You're doing a great job," Bill told Ronda.

Above was a hole in the jungle foliage on the other side of the trail.

"Can you throw one through that hole?" asked Bill.

"Yeah, I can do that," said Ronda.

"Do it," said Bill.

Ronda threw the grenade through the opening. After it exploded on the other side, they heard Vietnamese yelling and screaming. Bill always figured the American hand grenade was one of the most efficient weapons the infantry had. Unlike Chi-com grenades which exploded in chunks, the American grenades had one mile of fine segmented wire inside that exploded into thousands of tiny pieces, shredding whatever was in range. Bill thought that if he had been hit by an American grenade, instead of that Chi-com variety, he'd be dead right now, or neutered.

Lieutenant Haas motioned for Bill to come to him. Bill scrambled over to Haas who had been peppered in the face with shrapnel. One lens of Haas's glasses was shattered. Phillips, Haas's RTO, was seriously wounded in the leg, unconscious, pale, and in shock. Doc Christensen, who himself had frag wounds in his arms, was working on him.

Haas, who was on the radio, said "Bender says we're outnumbered. We got gunships coming in." He added "Belcher got knocked out. He's dead up there in the trail. I heard his gun go silent. I went up to see about him. He had a light pulse. I held his hand and he died. Go up there, get his body and that machine gun out of the trail. We all walked in here together. We're all going out together. We gotta do this pretty quick. The gunships are on the way."

Bill went to get Belcher. He told Ronda and Lovelace to come with him. When he got to the trail, he could see Belcher's body. His face, blackened by an explosion, at first made Bill think that one of their black soldiers had also been killed, and he had found him instead of Belcher. Then he recognized Belcher by a distinctive gold tooth. Bill pulled Belcher and the machine gun off the trail. He then dragged Belcher by the arm down the slope the 10 or 15 feet to where Lieutenant Haas was. They wrapped Frank in a poncho.

Haas told Bill "The gunships want us to mark the enemy's position with smoke grenades. But I'm afraid the NVA might throw them back at us."

"Let's throw frag grenades with the smoke grenades," Bill said. Haas agreed it was a good idea.

Haas sent Bill back up to the top of the slope to ready everyone for the grenade throw. At Haas's command of "Throw grenades" a volley of smoke and frag grenades flew across the trail. A few seconds later red, purple, and green smoke filled the air, intermixed with the explosions of multiple frag grenades. Once the smoke cleared the tree canopy, the gunships, now hovering overhead, opened up on the NVA with their Gatling guns, dissolving the trees like massive weed eaters.

Under the protection of a circling gunship, Second Platoon returned to Bingo carrying Belcher and Phillips in poncho litters, all the while hearing NVA troops yelling, screaming, and dying. Bill took rear security with Belcher's machine gun. Arnold Lovelace had been hit in the hand, but he stayed behind to help Bill. "I can still shoot an M-16 with one hand," Lovelace said.

Ten or 15 minutes later, with everybody back on Bingo, the place looked like the emergency room in a crowded hospital. Belcher was dead, and wounded were scattered throughout the area. Four medics were providing aid. They had started an IV on Phillips, the worst of the wounded, with shrapnel in his leg. Bolton had shrapnel wounds, and was shot in the ankle. Lovelace was shot in the left hand. Shrapnel had peppered Haas in the face. Others hit by shrapnel, some more seriously wounded than others, included Bridges, Sheppard, Davis, Billups, Lindsey, Boone, Michaels, Doc Christensen and of course, Bill.

Cliff Torrey came up to Bill. "Are you all right, Boe? Is there anything I can do for you?" he asked.

"I'm hungry," said Bill.

Torrey got Bill a can of Beanie Weenies. He told Bill those on the hill had been ordered to remain in place because the gunships would be coming, and they didn't want additional troops to add to any confusion as to who was where.

To ensure no one was left behind, Bender went among Second Platoon's wounded and other men taking an inventory of who was there. Haas surveyed the wounded to see how badly each man was hurt. Others maintained a Company perimeter in case the dinks attacked again. Lieutenant Haas congratulated everyone. "You guys did great," he said. Lieutenant Bender told them how worried those on the hill had been, and how proud they were of them for the battle they had fought.

Five minutes later a DUSTOFF came in to pick up the most seriously wounded, followed by others who took men out in accordance with the gravity of their wounds. Two gunships were still firing, chewing up the weeds, and mauling the NVA as they saturated the area with mini-gun and cannon fire.

Haas said the last medevac run was delayed because another platoon in another company had been hit. "You guys all right to stick around?" asked Haas. "We got another medevac coming in about 45 minutes." Those left were Bill, Ronda, Christensen, and Sheppard. They said they could wait.

When the last DUSTOFF came in to pick up the remaining four, Lieutenant Haas told Bill "Boe, I'm sending you guys out. I need to stay here and reorganize the Platoon. I hate to lose Frank. They say Phillips will be okay. I'll be waiting on you. Maybe you'll be back in a couple of weeks."

As the four climbed aboard the DUSTOFF, the pilot asked "How bad are you guys hit?"

"We're okay," said Bill

"We got jets coming in," said the pilot. "Since you guys aren't all that bad, you'll want to watch." The chopper went up high and hovered as two F-4 Phantoms came in and dropped napalm, creating a huge, rolling black and orange wave of fire that engulfed and vaporized the ambush area, including the packs the guys had to leave behind when they returned to Bingo. They didn't want NVA to gather munitions or personal information contained in those packs.

"That's pretty impressive," said the pilot.

"Yeah it is," said Sheppard.

After watching the napalm attacks, the pilot said ""I'm taking you guys to Polei Kleng." At Polei Kleng, the medics examined each man at the landing zone, and told the pilot to take them on to the 71st Evacuation Hospital in Pleiku.

Bob Lively of Reno, Nevada removes a leech from his leg while at LZ Bingo.

CHAPTER 33.
GETTING SHORT AND GOING HOME

Father Hagen met them as they got off the DUSTOFF at the hospital.

"What can I do for you?" he said.

"I could use something to drink. Maybe a Coke or a beer. And we haven't eaten since this morning before the ambush," said Sheppard.

Father Hagen checked with one of the medics. "Is there any reason these guys can't have something to eat and drink?"

"That'll be okay," said the medic.

Father Hagen sent his driver to get them something to eat. He came back in a few minutes with sandwiches and beer. Father Hagen continually looked out for the men.

Later that evening, a young female Army doctor came to attend to Bill. "You're going to need to take your clothes off," she said.

"All my clothes?" asked Bill.

"Yes, Sergeant," she said. "I've got to get the shrapnel out of you. I've seen it all. Seeing your butt will be nothing new to me."

After a few deadening shots of anesthesia, she used instruments to remove the shrapnel. Each time she removed a piece, Bill could hear the metallic noise it made when she dropped it into a metal receptacle. One piece about the size of a piece of buckshot was embedded very deep.

"Sergeant, I can cut muscle and go after this piece, or we can leave it where it is. It might be better to leave it than for me to dig deeper to get it out. What would you like for me to do?"

"Will it hurt to leave it there?" Bill asked her.

"Your body will form scar tissue around it, and it probably won't ever cause you a problem," she said. "But if I dig it out, I'll have to do a lot of cutting which might cause you a problem."

"Leave it there," said Bill.

After they all had surgery, Bill, Shep, and Christensen lay in their beds, still pumped with adrenalin from the ambush, unable to sleep. They went to the medic station, where they asked for coffee, which the medics provided. The three then went and sat in chairs outside, enjoyed their coffee, and discussed the day's events.

After three days, Bill and Christensen were airlifted to the 6th Convalescent Center in Cam Rahn Bay. While at Cam Rahn, Bill and Christensen each received the Purple Heart award. Although their packs stayed behind after the ambush, Bill, the would-be journalist, did manage to salvage his transistor radio and his Instamatic camera, both of which he still had with him. He and Christensen went outside for a photo of them with their new awards.

While in Cam Rahn, Bill had the opportunity to walk the beach. Soldiers recuperating are normally assigned duties. Since Bill was an NCO, however, he didn't have to pull duty, so strolling the beach was how he spent his free time. Christensen, a medic, made rounds with the other medics.

One day, while sipping a canteen Coke on the beach, Bill listened to country and western music on AFVN. He heard a new song by a new artist named Waylon Jennings, "Love of the Common People." Bill liked the song. It was about the America he believed in. He thought Jennings may have a career in music.

Another day Bill was sitting by his bed writing to Raelene when Stephen Forgey walked in.

"Sergeant Boe, I'm now here with you. I got wounded too," said Forgey.

"Good grief, Forgey, what happened?" said Bill.

"Three days after you left," said Forgey, "we got mortared. A round hit right on top of us. Boetje was killed. Rivera was killed. Winter was wounded and died the next day."

"Man, I hate to hear that," said Bill. "Those guys probably saved all of us. They were covering our right flank. If the NVA had gotten around us, they could have killed us all. Those guys were heroes, and nobody will ever know."

Bill and Forgey went to the canteen for a cup of coffee. There, they talked about life, and what they hoped to do when they got home.

Later, in his bed, Bill thought about his platoon. Of the 30 who went out of LZ Bingo's perimeter on the morning of 7 June, four had since been killed, and at least 14 were wounded. At most, only 12 were left in the field.

Less than a week later, Bill was discharged and airlifted back to Pleiku. Back at the Company Area, he ran into Warren Conner who was now assigned to driving a truck on supply convoys between Pleiku and Kontum. Bill also met the newly arrived First Sergeant, Sergeant Porterfied. Porterfield was a good man. A black guy from Alabama, he and Conner, a white guy from Georgia, had struck up a great friendship. Porterfield loved music. He especially liked Nat King Cole. He and Conner would sometimes sit around and sing along together to "Mona Lisa."

"We pretty good. Ain't we, Boe?" Porterfield said. "Me and Conner gonna be a salt-and-pepper duo back in Atlanta. We'll be famous."

Porterfield assigned Boe to be in charge of bunker and tower guards. After one day of dealing with the dope-smoking REMFs, Bill asked to be reassigned.

"Can I be Conner's door gunner?" Bill asked Porterfield.

"Well," said Porterfield, "there's no official position as truck door gunner. But the regs don't way we can't do it, so fine. You go ride with Conner."

Bill and Conner spent the next few weeks convoying in Conner's truck from Pleiku to Kontum, and back. It was easy duty. They'd go from Pleiku to Kontum one day. Sleep in the truck. Then, return to Pleiku the next. There was always danger of an ambush, but the convoys were heavily armed, and gunships accompanied them.

"It's safer on these convoys than being back home in Georgia," Conner told Bill.

Still, no one wanted to convoy too close to the big gasoline truck. Conner would position his truck to keep his distance. "I've been over here too long to end up as a fire ball," he said.

In Pleiku, Carpenter told Bill he needed to stick around the next few days to prepare to DEROS. After out-processing, which included a final medical check, and some dental work, he caught a flight to Cam Rahn Bay where he spent the night in the DEROS barracks. The next day, all those going back to the States rode a green Army bus with chicken wire on the windows to the airport.

On the tarmac was Bill's freedom bird—a chartered Continental airliner with stairs leading up to the door. Bill filed up to the plane, about midway in line, climbed the stairs, and found a seat next to Cleve Snodgrass from Tallahassee. He and Snodgrass, who was not in Second Platoon, were at Tiger Land together, and now they were on the same plane back to the States.

The big commercial jet taxied to its take-off point. The engines revved, pushing Bill slightly back in his seat. As the big bird lifted off and its landing gear retracted, people on the plane clapped. Bill did not. He thought about the guys he was leaving behind. He was glad to be going home in one piece, but part of him wanted to stay and help his buddies do the same. After a year in combat, he thought he might be able to help them survive. He had never had friendships like those he developed in Vietnam, where men depended on one another for their very lives.

The pilot came on the intercom and announced if they looked out the window, they'd see below Cam Rahn Bay and the Republic of Vietnam.

"Vietnam is behind us," he said. "Ahead of us is the United States of America. I'm taking you boys home."

At that point, over the intercom came Roger Williams's version of "Born Free." Bill choked up when he heard the song's words, especially the part about following your heart.

He still chokes up when he hears that song.

Bill (left) and Eddie Bolton at the 71st Evac Hospital in Pleiku after the ambush near Bingo

Bill and "Doc" Dennis Christensen at the Sixth Convalescent Center
in Cam Rahn Bay right after their Purple Heart ceremony.

EPILOGUE

During Bill's 30-day leave after returning from Vietnam, he visited his brother in Atlanta, where he purchased a 1968 red Pontiac GTO with a black vinyl roof. While driving from Pahokee to his newly assigned duty station at Fort Hood, Texas he stopped in Tallahassee and located the Alpha Omicron Pi sorority house. He knocked on the door. An attractive brunette peeked outside and asked "May I help you?" Bill responded, "You already have. You wrote me letters in Vietnam." The brunette yelled inside, "One of our soldiers is here!" Bill was immediately embraced by a dozen perfumed ladies who engulfed him with hugs and kisses. They invited him to stay for supper and instructed that he must wear his uniform. That evening, attired in his dress greens with two rows of ribbons, Bill was seated at the head table, flanked by Susie Wierengo and Robyn Ann Green. When introduced, 80 beautiful ladies from Florida, Alabama, and Georgia gave him a standing ovation. The war was over for Bill Boe, and he had received his own victory parade.

TRIBUTE TO THE FALLEN

Delta Company's history started in August of 1967 when it was formed at Duc Pho. From 1967 to 1970 Delta Company lost 34 men in Vietnam. The following pages pay tribute to each of them. As they rest in peace, may they rest assured they are not forgotten.

Spec. 4 Guadalupe Perez
Age 20
San Joaquin, California
17 September 1967
Quang Tin Province
Small Arms

Private First Class Gailen Cheek Crosslin
Age 20
Midwest City, Oklahoma
19 September 1967
Quang Tin Province
Friendly Fire, Mortar

Vietnam Veterans Memorial

DONALD W. HOLLENBACH

Private First Class Donald Walter Hollenbach
Age 20
Levittown, New York
22 November 1967
Quang Ngai Province
Small Arms

Spec. 4 James Strong Yoder
Age 18
Knoxville, Tennessee
22 November 1967
Quang Ngai Province
Small Arms

Vietnam Veterans Memorial

OMER P DICKERSON

Private First Class Omer Paul Dickerson
Age 20
Elsberry, Missouri
4 December 1967
Quang Ngai Province
Small Arms

Vietnam Veterans Memorial

WILLIAM D ORDWAY

Second Lieutenant William Dwight Ordway
Age 21
Baldwinville, Massachusetts
18 January 1968
Quang Ngai Province
Chi-com Grenade, Multiple Fragmentation Wounds

Vietnam Veterans Memorial

Private First Class Donald Lawrence Glover
Age 20
Pelham, Georgia
19 January 1968
Quang Ngai Province
"Bouncing Betty" Booby Trap

Vietnam Veterans Memorial

Spec. 4 Gregory Thomas Iding
Age 20
Cincinnati, Ohio
9 February 1968
Quang Nam Province
Small Arms

Vietnam Veterans Memorial

Spec. 4 Jose G. Cortez
Age 20
Corpus Christi, Texas
9 February 1968
Quang Nam Province
Mortar

Vietnam Veterans Memorial

Private First Class Norman Charles Kissinger
Age 22
Milwaukee, Wisconsin
9 February 1968
Quang Nam Province
Mortar

Private First Class James Garrett Miller
Age 21
Akron, Ohio
9 February 1968
Quang Nam Province
Mortar

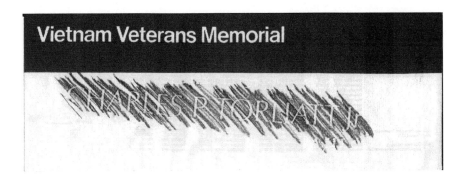

Private First Class Charles Peter Torliatt
Age 20
Petaluma, California
9 February 1968
Quang Nam Province
Mortar

Vietnam Veterans Memorial

Spec. 4 Robert Wayne Seaton
Age 22
Kevil, Kentucky
19 February 1968
Incident date 8 February 1968
Quang Nam Province
Multiple Fragmentation Wounds

Vietnam Veterans Memorial

Spec. 4 Steven Richard Anderson
Age 23
Levittown, New York
19 February 1968
Quang Nam Province
Small Arms

Vietnam Veterans Memorial

Private First Class Paul James Miller
Age 20
Poplar Bluff, Missouri
27 February 1968
Quang Nam Province
Friendly Fire – Airstrike

Spec. 4 William Henry Harff, Jr.
Age 23
Kenosha, Wisconsin
28 April 1968
Kontum Province
Mortar

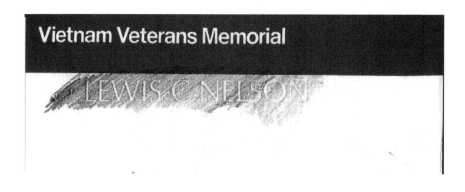

Vietnam Veterans Memorial

Spec. 4 Lewis Charles Nelson
Age 24
Seattle, Washington
28 April 1968
Kontum Province
Mortar

Vietnam Veterans Memorial

WILLIS G JONES

Spec. 4 Willis G. Jones
Age 20
Grand Rapids, Michigan
13 May 1968
Province Not Reported
Malaria

Vietnam Veterans Memorial

STEPHEN E CRAWFORD

Private First Class Stephen Earl Crawford
Age 18
Portsmouth, Ohio
16 May 1968
Kontum Province
Mortar

Vietnam Veterans Memorial

FRANK E BELCHER

Spec. 4 Frank Edward Belcher
Age 22
Osseo, Michigan
7 June 1968
Kontum Province
Multiple Fragmentation Wounds

Vietnam Veterans Memorial

Spec. 4 William Wayne Boetje
Age 19
Rock Island, Illinois
10 June 1968
Kontum Province
Mortar

Vietnam Veterans Memorial

Private First Class Julio Serrano-Rivera
Age 25
Mayaguez, Puerto Rico
10 June 1968
Kontum Province
Mortar

Vietnam Veterans Memorial

ROY A WINTER

Spec. 4 Roy Alan Winter
Age 20
Aurora, Missouri
11 June 1968
Incident Date 10 June 1968
Kontum Province
Mortar

Vietnam Veterans Memorial

JOHNNIE W ATOR

Sergeant Johnnie Wayne Ator
Age 20
Pittsfield, Illinois
9 February 1969
Pleiku Province
Small Arms

Vietnam Veterans Memorial

BOBBY GENE GAMBLE

Corporal Bobby Gene Gamble
Age 21
Richard City, Tennessee
9 February 1969
Pleiku Province
Small Arms

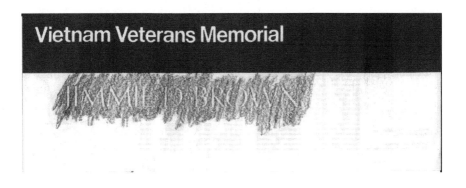

Vietnam Veterans Memorial

Spec. 4 Jimmie Donovan Brown
Age 21
Detroit, Michigan
16 October 1969
Pleiku Province
Friendly Fire – Artillery

Vietnam Veterans Memorial

Staff Sergeant Michael Kenneth Sawyer
Age 22
Norfolk, Virginia
16 October 1969
Pleiku Province
Friendly Fire – Artillery

Vietnam Veterans Memorial

BRADLEY J LOGAN

Private First Class Bradley John Logan
Age 20
Dearborn, Michigan
6 November 1969
Pleiku Province
Multiple Fragmentation Wounds

Vietnam Veterans Memorial

RAYMOND C FOERSTER

Spec. 4 Raymond Carl Foerster
Age 21
Dallas, Texas
6 November 1969
Pleiku Province
Multiple Fragmentation Wounds

Vietnam Veterans Memorial

DAVID J GAMBLE

Corporal David John Gamble
Age 23
Ellwood City, Pennsylvania
6 November 1969
Pleiku Province
Rocket

Vietnam Veterans Memorial

Spec. 4 Donald Gene Hedgecock
Age 21
Cahokia, Illinois
6 November 1969
Pleiku Province
Multiple Fragmentation Wounds

Vietnam Veterans Memorial

RONALD L DELONG

Corporal Ronald Lawrence De Long
Age 22
Collegedale, Tennessee
6 November 1969
Pleiku Province
Multiple Fragmentation Wounds

Vietnam Veterans Memorial

RICHARD A MOIREN

Sergeant Richard Allen Moiren
Age 21
Mobile, Alabama
24 April 1970
Binh Dinh Province
Small Arms

Vietnam Veterans Memorial

DOUGLAS H SILVERNAIL

Staff Sergeant Douglas Harold Silvernail
Age 21
Bloomfield, New York
7 October 1970
Binh Dinh Province
Booby Trap